L. Walter Arnold

I Remember

The Way Things Used To Be

First Edition

L. Walker Arnold

ARNOLD
PUBLICATIONS
Nicholasville, KY 40356

I Remember
The Way Things Used To Be
Published by Arnold Publications

First Edition, August, 1994

Cover Art by L. Walker Arnold

Library of Congress Card Number: 94-094499
ISBN: 0-9629688-4-6

Printed in the United States of America

Arnold Publications
2440 Bethel Road
Nicholasville, KY 40356

Phone (800) 854-8571

*Dedicated to the memory of Edward Lawrence Arnold
and Texie Agee Arnold, my father and mother,
whose exemplary examples and teachings
taught me the value of hard work,
right living, and integrity.*

CONTENTS

The Good Old Days

L. Walker Arnold

I long for the good old days,
  When a man's word was his bond,
And a handshake sealed a deal
  As good as the touch of a magic wand.

I long for the days when a dirty word
  Made one blush and look askance.
And Mama threatened to wash with soap
  That dirty mouth when she got a chance.

Back then, girls were sweet and innocent,
  And as pure as the driven snow,
So we placed them on a pedestal,
  And hoped our crudeness wouldn't show.

Now the good old days have passed me by.
  It's almost like they'd never been,
But I can never forget those days
  When ladies were ladies and men were
    men.

Chapter 1
Clearing Away the Brush

*I*t seems only yesterday that I was a barefoot boy, chasing a hoop down a dusty, country road. Now they call me a senior citizen. Someone has said there are four stages in a man's life. There is the stage when ladies look at him and say, "My, isn't he cute." A few years later, the girls look at him and sigh, "Oh, isn't he handsome." Then there comes the stage when his peers look at him and say, "You're looking good." What they really mean is, "You look better than I thought you would at your age." Then there is the time when people look at a man and say, "He looks natural."

I can hardly believe that I have reached the stage in life when my peers tell me I'm looking good, and children look up at me and say, "Gee, he's old." I don't feel old, but I'll have to admit that a lot of water has gone under the bridge since that country boy chased that hoop down the road.

I have seen many changes in my lifetime. I started life in horse-and-buggy days. Now we travel in jet aircraft and send men into space. My father used to hoot at the suggestion that men would one day go to the moon in a rocket. I have lived to see men walk on the moon!

When I was a boy, we used to stand on the hill in front of our house and call to our neighbor on the next hill at the top of our voices. Now we communicate by radio transmitters, cellular phones, fax machines, E-mail, and voice mail. We even see what is happening on the other side of the earth by way of satellite and television.

I started life in a house that was dimly lit by kerosene lamps. Now our houses and our cities blaze with electric lights. We used to write, figure and keep records by dipping scratchy pens in bottles of ink and dragging them across pages that had to be blotted from time to time and usually looked messy when we finished with them. Now those of us who are computer literate do all our writing, figuring, and record keeping with computers.

In my lifetime we have progressed in heating our homes, from the fireplace to the furnace, to solar heat and to heat pumps. In entertainment, we have gone from the victrola, with the big morning-glory horn, to CD players, tape players, radio, television, and VCR recorders. Motion pictures used to be flickering black and white images, projected on a silver screen. The film was highly flammable and often caught fire during projection. The pictures were silent, so one had to read the messages projected on the screen to know what the characters were saying. Now we have televisions in our homes that bring us news and entertainment with color pictures and sound.

My generation has seen more change than any generation in history. Sadly, those of us who have lived to see so many changes are now a dying generation, and the memory of how people lived before those changes will die with us. So, with some trepidation, I have decided to chronicle a few memories of those changes in this book. I trust it will help my own generation to remember how it used to be, and that it will give those who come after us an idea of the days through which we have lived.

This book is largely autobiographical, for I cannot write about my memories without writing about my life. Many have asked me to write my life's story, but until now I have deferred to do so. First, I have declined to write my life story because I have felt that much of it would not make interesting reading. Second, there are some things I have no desire to tell. Third, I do not wish to take credit for anything I have accomplished, nor do I want to parade my failures. However, I do feel at liberty to relate some selected memories from my long and extremely busy lifetime.

Some of the material in this book has been previously published in *The Arnold Report*, under the caption, *I Remember*. The memories I have shared in *The Arnold Report* were so well received, I have decided that they should be enlarged upon and preserved in more permanent form. I hope that in this form these memories will be enjoyed by more people and by future generations.

This book could be called my memoirs. It is that—somewhat. It could be called the history of my time, for it does contain a bit of the history of the years through which I have lived. This book is somewhat a record of the discoveries and inventions of the twentieth century, for the years of my lifetime have been the greatest years of discovery and invention in the history of the world.

This book could be called a book of nostalgia, for it harks back to a quieter, simpler time that so many of us like to recall. I trust that it will stimulate the imagination of my readers, and that many will enjoy wandering down the trails of memory with me. I trust also that the younger generation will take pleasure in reading *The Way Things Used To Be.*

Chapter 2

The Miracle of My Birth

I was born in the little village of Buckeye, Kentucky, January 17, on a cold, winter day, according to my mother. That was more years ago than I care to remember, but I find many people who are wondering how old I am. I wonder why. I'm the one who should be concerned about that.

To those who are curious about my age, I will only say what I said to a nosy school teacher when I was in the first grade. Or was it the second? The teacher asked me when I was born, and I promptly replied, "I do not remember." Then I wondered why everyone in the classroom laughed.

For those who are not satisfied with that answer, I will say that I can remember the Vietnam War, the Korean Conflict, WWII and some talk of WWI, but, try as I will, I cannot remember the Civil War.

I was born the son of Edward Lawrence Arnold and Texie Agee Arnold. My father was a village blacksmith at the time of my birth, but he later became a farmer and remained one until he retired at the age of seventy-two.

My mother was a simple Christian housewife who had never heard of "Women's Lib." She would not have been interested if she had, for she was already as liberated as she could be. She was free to love her husband, her child, and her home. She was free to read her Bible, to pray, and to attend church. She was free to be a homemaker, and she never dreamed of being a homebreaker. She was free to love her neighbors and to share what she had with them. She was free to bring her son to know the Lord, free to train him, free to pray for him, and free to instill in him the desire to serve God and to amount to something in the world. So she had no need of "Women's Lib."

Now, lest I get ahead of myself, it is best that I go back to the beginning of the story.

My mother, Texie, was one of three daughters born to Ferris and Emily Masters Agee. Her sisters were Lena and Ina. She was born in Madison County, Kentucky, but her family soon moved to Garrard County, where she grew up. She attended a country church with her family, and became a Christian at an early age.

From the time she was saved, Texie wanted to do something definite for the Lord. There were things she knew she could not do, for her education was limited, and she was not strong in body. She prayed about what she was to do, and finally she decided that the Lord wanted her to be a wife and the mother of a baby boy that would become a preacher. She surrendered her life for that purpose, and, like Hannah of old, she promised that if ever she had a son, she would dedicate him to the Lord. That decision became the guiding principle of her life.

In time, Edward Lawrence Arnold came courting at the Agee home, as young men did in those days. He did not drive up in an automobile, honk the horn in front of the house and wait for Texie to come out. Instead, he rode up on horseback, dismounted and hitched his horse at the stile. He crossed the stile and went to the front door and knocked.

As was the custom in those days, Texie's mother probably opened the door and invited Ed to come in and have a seat. "Texie will be ready in a few minutes," she probably said.

Ed must have thanked her and entered the parlor and sat down.

Texie had most likely been ready and waiting for some time, but in those days it was thought proper to keep a young man waiting a decent length of time.

In due time Texie came into the parlor and the young couple greeted. As was the custom, Texie's mother retired to a room not too far away, while the young couple courted in the old-fashioned parlor.

Somebody has said that back then, the old mantle clock with the swinging pendulum seemed to say, "Take your time. Take your time."

At a later day, the alarm clock ticking on the dresser seemed to say, "Get together quick. Get together quick." Now we have silent clocks, except when they alarm. Then they only make a strange beeping sound, so they really don't say anything. The television is not silent though, and it often blasts away with the home-destroying message that young couples need not even bother with getting married.

It was a different world when Ed and Texie used to sit in the parlor together or ride their horses to the church on Sundays. Texie rode a sidesaddle, and she wore a riding habit that was long enough to cover her ankles, lest young men see too much. Now it seems the fear is that they will see too little.

Despite the restrictions of those days, somehow the courting got done, and in due time the man who was to be my father proposed to the girl who was to be my mother. I know not whether it was in the old parlor or in some shaded nook where they stopped their horses on the way to church. I only know that one day he said, "Wilt thou?" and she said, "I wilt."

In due time they married and moved into a little house across the road from the Baptist Church at Buckeye, Kentucky, where Ed had his blacksmith shop.

Blacksmithing was not an easy way to make a living, but he was not afraid of hard work. Yet, despite his hard work, the blacksmith shop did not prosper. He was softhearted and easy going, and he could not turn down those who wanted their horses shod or their farm tools mended on credit. Times were hard, and payments for services done on credit were slow. Ed could seldom bring himself to the point of asking that an account be paid, so all too often they remained unpaid.

That was not the only worry Texie had. Ed was not a Christian, and she must have had many a heartache as she prayed for a husband who was more interested in drinking and gambling than he was in going to church. Ed did not pray, but he swore easily and often.

However, Texie had one thing to cheer her during the first year of her marriage. She believed that she would soon fulfill her promise to the Lord by bearing a son who would become a preacher.

At last the day arrived, and she gave birth to a baby boy, but, to her sorrow, he was born dead. Her sorrow was made even greater when the doctor told her she could never bear another child and live. Her only recourse was to go to the Lord in prayer. In time the conviction grew that, no matter what the doctor had said, the Lord wanted her to be the mother of a preacher. So she prayed that the Lord would give her another baby boy, and that he would live.

In due time another baby boy was born to my mother, and he lived. She named him Louis Walker Arnold. It was a miracle that I was born alive. In my mother's lifetime she gave birth to three baby boys. Only one of them lived. The baby born before me was born dead, and the baby boy born after me was born dead. So it was a miracle that I lived.

After I was born, my mother was confined to her bed for many days. Years afterward, she told me that she had crawled to my crib on her hands and knees as soon as she was able and had buried her face in my body and wept. With tears streaming down her cheeks, she dedicated me to God.

When I was growing up, my mother prayed for me faithfully, and taught me the Word of God. I do not remember when I did not know that the Bible is the Word of God. Nor can I remember when I did not know that I needed to be saved. My bedtime stories were from the Bible, and my lullabies were the old hymns. To this day I can hear my mother singing as she went about the house, *I Come to the Garden Alone.* I love that song to this day.

My mother prayed for me until God saved me. Then she prayed until I answered the call to preach. After I was in the ministry, she continued to pray for me. She prayed for me as long as she lived, and I believe that in Heaven she is still praying for me.

(Chapter 3)
The Devil Wanted Me Dead

*M*y birth was a miracle, but my battle for life was not over. While I was yet an infant, an epidemic of smallpox swept our community, and I came down with that dreaded, killer disease. I was not expected to live, but I did.

Also in my infancy, I had a disease called scrofula, a swelling in the neck caused by tuberculosis of the lymph nodes in that area. I was sick for a long time and suffered a great deal, I was told when I was old enough to understand. Finally the doctor decided to lance my neck. He must have come close to cutting my head off, for a scar on my neck remains to this day. I may have come close to dying, but I did not.

As a boy growing up, I was skinny and delicate, and I was frequently ill with the usual childhood diseases. I also had several bouts with appendicitis in my preteen years. It is strange that they never rushed me to surgery. I spent many days in bed with my knees drawn up against my stomach to ease the pain, and there were frequent times of nausea. It is also strange that my appendix did not rupture. If it had, I would most likely have died. I never had an operation for my diseased appendix, but somehow I lived through the pain and suffering, and eventually I got over it. Satan wanted me dead, ". . . *but God meant it unto good . . ."*

Between my bouts of sickness, I was very active. I ran and jumped and played like other boys, and I spent long hours exercising and trying to build up my health. Somewhere I had heard that President Teddy Roosevelt had been delicate in health as a boy and that through exercise he had built a robust body and abounding health. So I exercised whenever I was able to do so.

By the time I reached my teen years, my health was better, so Satan tried different tactics. He tried to get me killed. One night I went hunting with my dogs, carrying a lantern as I always did. It was the custom back then to hunt on neighboring farms without prior notice, so with no thought of danger, I climbed a fence and started across a neighbor's farm. I had hunted on this farm before, both alone and in company with other boys my age. Never had this farmer, or any other farmer in the community for that matter, offered the least objection to our hunting on their land. But on this night, I saw a light go on in the farmhouse, and a moment later someone raised a window and fired two shots at me in quick succession. Bullets thudded into the ground at my feet. It didn't take me long to get over the fence and away from this neighbor's farm. Satan wanted me dead, "... *but God* ..."

Before television, or even radio, young people often met in a home to have a party. A party back then did not mean drinking liquor or shooting dope, though some roughnecks did sometimes go outside and take a nip of "moonshine" from a fruit jar. A party in those days was for playing games, telling stories, asking and answering riddles, making pull candy, laughing, playing music and singing. This was one of the favorite ways young people had of entertaining themselves.

One night, as a friend and I were walking home from a party, a young man waylaid us and shot at us twice. I heard the bullets whiz past me, and I heard them thud into a high bank beside the side the road. They only missed me by inches. Satan wanted me dead," ... *but God* ..."

I thought I knew who had done the shooting, so the next day I went to see him. "Here are the two shells you wasted shooting at me last night," I said, offering them to him. He didn't take the shells, but he didn't deny shooting at me either.

About this time, a young man came to our farm and started a fight with me. My mother had taught me to never start a fight, but never to run if one could not be avoided. The young man decided that he should do the running, and I called after him to never come back on our property again. This may not have been the right thing to do. I am just telling the way it happened.

Soon he came back looking for trouble. I did

not know he was hiding an open knife behind him when he started the fight. I did not back off, and he struck for my heart with the knife. The blade of the knife went through my lumber jacket directly over my heart. I was turning as it struck, so the knife went through my under jacket a bit lower. The hole it cut in my shirt was still lower. The blade went through my underwear directly above my lower rib. It cut through the flesh and hit the rib bone. That stopped it from penetrating the cavity of my body. If his knife had hit where he aimed it, I would have died on the spot. Adam's rib gave him a wife. My rib saved my life. Satan wanted me dead, "... *but God* ..."

After I had grown-up and gone into the ministry, I had more illnesses. In one year I had typhoid fever, whooping cough, and kidney stones. (Imagine a grown man having whooping cough.) About that time I also had mumps, but all that was not the worse of my sickness. I also had to have my tonsils taken out. The doctor took them out with me sitting on a stool in his office. He put a shot in my throat to numb the pain, but it had no effect. I thought he was cutting my head off while he was taking my tonsils out. Somehow I lived through the pain. I recovered without the doctor seeing me again.

Shortly after that, a doctor discovered that I had Bright's disease—at that time incurable. I'm sure they have another name for it now. The doctor frankly told me that I did not have long to live. I did not believe him, so I went to another doctor. He gave me the same diagnosis. Still unbelieving, I went from doctor to doctor. (It was fortunate for me that doctors didn't charge preachers in those days.) I visited at least seven doctors, and only one of them gave me any hope. He treated me for some time. Then one day he told me he had done all he could for me, and I was not improving.

"You will only live a short time," he told me. "I suggest that you quit the ministry. Go out West and take it easy. Enjoy the little time you have left. It won't be long."

I walked out of his office feeling that I had received a death sentence. I did not question what he had told me, for by that time the disease had so ravished my body, it was evident that I was dying. I only weighed 123 pounds, and I was so weak I could barely walk from my parsonage across a small lawn to the front door of my church and down the aisle to the pulpit. By the time I had preached 15 minutes, I was completely exhausted, and it was all I could do to get back to the parsonage and go to bed. I had to rest all afternoon to be able to preach that night. I was almost too weak to drive my automobile, and when I did drive my vision often blacked out. It is a wonder I was not killed in an accident. Satan wanted me dead," . . . *but God . . .*"

I will never know where I got the faith to pray for my healing, unless it was from a book I read on healing about that time. I only know that one dark night, about two o'clock in the morning, I called in another doctor.

I had not slept. I was so weak I could barely get out of bed and on my knees. I remember praying something like this: "Dear Lord, You have called me to preach, and I do not believe my ministry is over. My doctor has told me to quit the ministry, but I don't believe You want me to quit. Lord, I can't go on preaching the way I am, so I pray that You will heal me. I don't care whether You give me new kidneys or repair the ones I have. I just want You to heal me."

I didn't hear any bells or whistles, but a sense of peace came to my heart, and a feeling of well-being came to my body. I got back into bed, fell asleep, and slept like a baby until the next morning. When I awoke, I felt better than I had in months. I decided to forget the restricted diet I was on and eat like a normal person. Eating must have agreed with me, for I started gaining weight almost at once. According to a record I kept of answered prayers back then, I gained 32 pounds in the next month. I recall that by that time I was feeling great. Nonetheless, I decided to go to a specialist for a checkup. The specialist ran his tests, then told me to go for a walk and to come back in about an hour. When I returned, he gave me good news.

"I don't know what you have had, but there is nothing wrong with you now," he said.

I left his office thanking and praising God for health to go on with my ministry. Satan wanted me dead, "... *but God* ..."

Chapter 4
Boyhood Days

I grew up on a rock-strewn, gully-washed hill farm with a weathered barn and a crude little house, but I still found much beauty to enjoy. There were summer mornings when the sun came up like a golden lamp and turned the dewdrops on the meadows, the morning glories, and the trumpet flowers into diamonds. At high noon the sunbeams danced on the riffles of the creek, and in the evening they painted the western sky in shades of pink and red and gold. When rain clouds appeared, the sun painted a rainbow across them.

The creek at the foot of the hill was filled with minnows and tadpoles. The pool below the house was the home of green and brown bullfrogs. Snake doctors darted in the air around the pool and along the creek, and butterflies danced in the air above Mama's flower garden in the side yard.

In winter the farm was often covered with a blanket of snow. The snow formed a canvas for the frost to display its diamonds upon, and the winter sun came up to make them blaze with light. I often looked out at the frost diamonds through icicles that hung like great snaggled teeth from the eaves of our house.

Springtime was fresh with promise when the buttercups bloomed. A bit later, the peach and plum and apple trees hung out their blossoms.

In the fall the hickory and walnut trees were loaded with nuts, and the maple, oak, and beech trees, turned red and gold and yellow and brown and rust. They shook their heads in the autumn wind, and their leaves drifted downward like tiny sails.

When I was growing up, I seldom crossed the borders of our county. The only times I did were when my grandmother took me to Richmond, in Madison County, in her buggy. But there was always enough for me to see and enjoy in my own neighborhood.

In manhood, I have seen mighty oceans rocking in their beds, restless, beautiful, and terrible. I have seen great rivers flowing through verdant valleys, with mighty mountains above them, stabbing at the clouds. I have seen smoking volcanoes under cloud-fleeced skies, wildflower gardens blossoming in tropical jungles, and birds, plumed with feathers of every hue, darting and wheeling through tangled trees and vines. But nothing I have seen holds more for me in memory than the old home place.

In my growing up years, we knew nothing of toast for breakfast, salad for lunch, and dinner in the evening. At breakfast time we ate ham, red-eye gravy, eggs, and hot biscuits, with blackberry jam, apple jelly, or sorghum. At noon, in the summertime, we ate fried chicken from our own flock. In the fall, during the hunting season, we killed rabbits and ate them for dinner or supper. In the spring, before our chickens came on, we hunted and shot young rabbits, even though it was out of season.

In the winter we ate steak or pork, from animals we had raised on the farm. In the early spring we went wild-greens picking on our farm and on neighboring farms. A bit later we had onions, lettuce and radishes from our early garden, and from rows we had planted along the edge of the tobacco beds. When the summer garden came on, we had "taters" and beans, "maters" and corn and squash. Also, we had butter beans, green beans and melons in season. We always had biscuits or cornbread with our meals. We had coffee and milk, the year around, and in the summertime, we had iced tea to drink, if the ice we had brought from town on Saturday had not all melted.

Supper was a special time. We had finished the hard work for the day and fed the animals, milked the cow, gathered the eggs from the nests, and carried water from the spring. After that, we could relax and enjoy a good meal Mama had prepared.

When Mama finished cooking supper, she moved the kerosene lamp from the shelf to the center of the table. We always ate our supper by lamplight because electricity had not yet reached our community. When Mama set our plates on the table and put the food on, we all drew up our chairs and sat down to eat.

After we finished eating, Mama removed the dishes and food from the table. Then she brought the family Bible to the table. Sometimes Papa read aloud from the Bible, though he did not read very well. Usually Mama read to Papa and me. I liked it better when Mama read. After the Bible reading was finished, we usually remained at the table for a time, talking about what had been read. Often one of us would raise a question, and we would try to come up with an answer. I learned much from the Bible in this way, and by the time I was grown, I had a general knowledge of what the Bible was about.

When bedtime came, Mama picked up the lamp and led the way to my bedroom. She placed the lamp on the mantle, then knelt beside me while I said my bedtime prayer. After I had prayed, she would go out, promising to come back and tuck me in after I got in bed. I will never forget her good night kiss and the way she pulled the cover up around my shoulders. After she left with the lamp, it seemed that angels came down and hovered around my bed. I doubt that my mother realized that she was building memories that would last a lifetime.

One of the happiest memories of my child-hood was fishing in the nearby ponds and creeks. Papa first took me fishing when I was a small boy. He had been promising to take me for some time, and finally he set an afternoon when we would go. I am sure that as we worked in the field that morning, I must have reminded him several times of his promise.

After dinner I went out with Papa to make preparations to go fishing. Our preparations were simple and primitive, but I could not have been more excited. Money was scarce in those days, so instead of buying fishing tackle, we made our own.

We went to the cane thicket, a quarter mile from the house, and cut the tallest canes we could find for fishing poles. Then we made fishing lines from some of Mama's #9 sewing thread. We made the line by twisting the thread and doubling it a couple of times to make it strong enough to land the fish we hoped to catch. We made hooks of bent pins. We found small stones and tied them to the lines for sinkers, and we used short sections of pith from last year's cornstalk for floaters (bobbers). After we finished making our fishing tackles and wound the lines on our cane poles, we got an empty tin can and a grubbing hoe and went to dig for worms.

We were only going to fish for one afternoon, but Papa dug enough worms for a week of fishing. I was so eager to start fishing, I thought we would never reach the creek, but we finally did. Then, carrying the can of worms and our fishing poles, Papa led the way. We soon came to a fence near the creek and climbed it, and Papa continued to a likely spot on the creek bank. There he unwound my line, baited my hook and threw the line out in the water as far as he could with the short cane pole.

"Now watch the floater," he told me. "If it starts bobbing up and down, jerk the pole and you'll catch a fish."

He had scarcely finished his instructions when my bobber started bouncing in the water. My heart almost stopped, and I jerked the pole as hard as I could. If the tackle had been sufficient, and if I had been strong enough, I would have landed a whale, if one had been on the hook. As it was, I threw a tiny catfish over the fence and into the field behind me.

I scrambled over the fence and retrieved my tiny fish, and Papa cut a willow switch and strung the little fish on it and fastened it to the creek bank. The fish disappeared beneath the water at once, but I soon pulled it up for another look. I was sure there had never a more beautiful fish than the one I had caught. In manhood, I have fished in rivers, lakes and oceans. I have fished from shores, bridges, boat docks and boats. I have caught game fish, some of them large, but I have never had a bigger thrill fishing than I did the day I caught my first fish.

Papa and I fished often after that, and we caught far larger fish than my first one. I also fished alone and in the company of others my age. We fished in ponds, creeks and in a rock quarry. Often I caught a stringer full of tiny sunfish, and, late in the afternoon, I proudly carried them home. I cleaned the tiny fish, and Mama fried them for supper. She always fried them crisp and brown so we could eat them bones and all.

I still enjoy fishing, though I seldom have time or opportunity to fish these days. Long since, the business of my life has been fishing for men. I have had some great thrills in catching fish, but they do not compare with the thrill of catching men. I am thankful that my dad taught me to fish for fish. I am even more thankful that my Savior has taught me how to catch men. Jesus said to his disciples, ". . . *from henceforth thou shalt catch men*" (Luke 5:10). Again He said to them, ". . . *Follow me, and I will make you fishers of men*" (Matthew 4:19). Fishing for men has been my calling and my life's work, and I believe that all I experienced in my childhood and young manhood helped to prepare me for my life's work.

Chapter 5

I Knew Hard Times

*W*hen I was growing up, they said that times were hard, but we didn't start a riot, nor did we ask the government to support us. The government didn't have a poverty program in those days, but we had our own. We worked!

Among other things, we raised a garden. We ate from it in the summer, and canned enough from it to last through the winter. Besides the garden, we raised hogs and calves. We butchered enough hogs to keep us in meat for much of the year. From the hogs we also made lard. From the excess grease we made soap. We usually butchered a calf in the winter and feasted on choice steak and roast until it was gone.

Our cows kept us in sweet milk, clabber milk, butter, and buttermilk. We even made our own cottage cheese, and we made ice cream in the summertime, when we could get 50 cents to buy a 50 pound block of ice. We hauled the ice from town, wrapped in a gunnysack and tied on the bumper of our car, that is, after we finally got a car.

We raised chickens, so we had both eggs and chickens to eat. Mama sometimes raised turkeys for us to eat at Thanksgiving and Christmas.

For variety, we hunted and killed rabbits, and sometimes squirrels to eat. After I was old enough to have a 22 rifle, I learned to be a good shot so I would not waste 22 cartridges. After all they cost one half a cent each. Sometimes Papa, a good shot with a twelve gage shotgun, went hunting for quails. He usually brought home enough for a meal, and what a feast we would have.

There was no shortage of fish in the river, and in the summertime we caught enough fish to furnish many a good meal. We hardly realized that times were hard, though the hard times did make a good topic of conversation. We just knew there was a shortage of money. When we sold our crops, they did not bring much. Animals we sold often did not bring enough to pay the feed bill, but we got by. To get some spending money when I was a boy, I collected and sold scrap iron in the summertime, and I trapped and caught fur-bearing animals in the winter. I also caught fur-bearing animals by hunting with my dogs at night.

Every Saturday, Mama sold some cream and eggs and sometimes a pound of butter she had churned. From these she got enough money to buy the staples at the store. If there was money left over, she saved it against the day she would have to buy me some school clothes and books.

The weekly newspaper told of people out of work in other places, but that did not affect us.

We always had plenty of work to do. We met people in town who talked about hard times, about men out of work, and about people standing in breadlines. That was hard for us to understand, for we never had to go hungry. We were just short of money, and that was probably good for us, for it taught us to work hard, to be self-reliant, and to trust in God.

Around the first of July, after crops were laid-by, blackberries ripened in the briar patches on uncultivated hillsides and along creek bottoms. The berries were black, sweet, and juicy, and, though the chiggers were waiting to eat us alive, we went berry picking anyway.

The June bugs had already discovered the berries and were gorging themselves on the choicest of them. Every so often, while we were busy picking, one of them would take to flight with a sudden buzz, like a small plane taking off. The unexpected sound was always startling.

Before the day of berry picking ended, I always caught one of the largest June bugs to play with. The June bug looked like a Japanese beetle, though I never heard of a Japanese beetle when I was a boy. The June bug was the same shape and color as the Japanese beetle, but it was more than twice as large. The June bug was not nearly as destructive as its smaller cousin.

I wonder what ever happened to June bugs. I haven't seen one in years. For that matter, what happened to jar flies? They have been almost absent in our part of the country for a number of years. Remember how they used to buzz in the trees? You couldn't hear yourself think for them. Isn't it strange that we have not heard a word about them being an endangered species.

But back to the June bugs.

When we got home, I tied a string to one of the back legs of the June bug and released him so he could fly. He took off, buzzing like a small electric fan. Checked by the thread, he flew around and around, but he didn't go anywhere. I was holding the other end of the string, so all he could do was to buzz!

That brings to my mind several random thoughts.

Just as I controlled the June bug, the devil has a lot of people on a string, and they can no more free themselves than the June bug could. Like him, they do a lot of buzzing, but they're not going anywhere.

Only God can make a June bug, and only God can make blackberries for June bugs and people to eat.

When June bugs are gone, they are gone forever. When people leave this life, they live on—forever—somewhere. June bugs don't have a choice about their future, but people do. What people do about Jesus Christ will determine where they will be in eternity.

Another way we coped with hard times was to put up nuts in the fall of the year. Putting up nuts was more fun than working. After the first heavy frost had done its magic, and the trees had put on the colors of fall, it was time to go nut hunting. Most times, Papa, Mama, and I went nut hunting together. We left the house carrying a sack and headed for the big hickory tree, a quarter mile away. Our dogs, as excited as I was, ranged ahead, and with bounding heart, I ran after them. I did not stop running until I reached the big hickory tree. The dogs soon came to me, out of breath and panting.

The leaves on the hickory tree were lemon yellow. The other trees were bright yellow and gold and rust and brown and red. The nuts on the hickory tree had brown shells. Some nuts had fallen to the grown and lay half hidden in fallen leaves. Some of the shells had burst open.

I ran through the leaves and sent them flying with my feet. I pushed the nuts out of the way, piled up a great pile of leaves, fell in them and rolled in them. The dogs came to lie in the leaves, stretched full-length and panted happily.

When Mama and Papa arrived, we set to work picking up the fallen nuts, shelling them, and putting them in the sack. After we had picked up all the nuts we could find, Papa climbed the tree and shook off all that were loose. Then he climbed back down and helped Mama and me finish filling the sack.

When we finished, Papa threw the sack across his shoulder, and we went home. We put the nuts in a dry place to cure, thankful that they had cost us nothing. We did not even have to pay tax on them.

Usually we did not bring the nuts out until the week before Thanksgiving. Then, one night after supper, we all sat in the kitchen and cracked nuts and picked out enough kennels to make a hickory nut cake and my favorite dish, chocolate pudding with hickory nuts and raisins in it.

Mama usually baked the nut cake a day or two before Thanksgiving. While it was baking, she would not allow anyone to walk in the kitchen for fear it would fall (would not rise properly). The baking cake would fill the house with a delicious aroma. Mama usually cooked my favorite pudding, made with nuts and raisins, on Thanksgiving morning.

On Thanksgiving Day, we all arose early, and Mama cooked breakfast. We ate hurriedly, then Papa and I went to the barn to feed and milk. When we returned to the house, Mama would send me to the woodpile to bring an extra supply of wood for the grate and the kitchen range. Then I would go to the spring and carry water to the house by the bucket load. By the time I finished bringing in the water, the kitchen was warmed by the fire in the range, and Mama was mixing, stirring, preparing a half dozen dishes, and making bread. Meanwhile, Papa had gone out and caught a big turkey gobbler or rooster to be dressed and made ready for the oven.

Soon the house was filled with the wondrous aroma of food cooking. I will never forget those smells. Nor will I ever forget the food and the time at the table on Thanksgiving Day. That was a great time to be thankful and to enjoy the food. We had so much to eat for Thanksgiving, we forgot to remember that times were hard.

Chapter 6
Making My Own Toys

*B*ecause of the shortage of money, my parents and grandparents gave me few store-bought toys when I was growing up. About the most they gave me, except at Christmastime, was an occasional rubber ball or a top. At Christmas, Mama and Papa did stuff the stocking I hung by the fireplace with candy, nuts, and some small trinkets. And there was always an inexpensive toy or two.

In those days people did not give many gifts for Christmas, and most people observed Christmas in honor of the Lord's birth. Even the Christmas programs at school were centered around the birth of Jesus. So I knew what Christmas was about, but that did not keep me from enjoying the gifts and the giving at Christmas. Much of my excitement at that time of the year may have been because I was young, but I am sure that not having much the rest of the year also contributed to it.

Christmas toys usually did not last long, and when they were broken or worn-out, I had to start improvising as I had before. Like many boys of that era, I learned to make my own toys. They were the best anyway, for there was the fun of making them as well as the fun of playing with them.

I even learned to make my own marbles. Some boys won their marbles by playing "for keeps." I was a good marble shot, and I could easily have won marbles that way, but I knew I would get a whipping if I did and Mama or Papa found out about it. Besides, I soon developed scruples of my own, and I did not want to do anything dishonest.

The only other way I could get marbles, unless I found them or someone gave them to me, was to make them. Making marbles was a tricky business with only mediocre success. Nonetheless, I did make my marbles on some occasions. The way I made marbles was to get some good clay from a clay bank near our house. I still remember selecting clay that was just the right consistency and with the right moisture content. I pinched off the proper amount of clay and rolled it between the palms of my hands until it was smooth and round. I repeated the process until I had made as many round balls of clay as I wanted. Then I took them to the grate in the house and placed them in the glowing embers, being careful not to flatten them in the process.

The marbles had to be left in the fire until they baked as hard as bricks. After that I raked them from the fire and let them cool. That was a lot of work for marbles of poor quality, but I played with them until I could get better marbles.

I do not recall owning a football until I was in high school, but there were other kinds of balls. There were baseballs, hard rubber balls, hollow rubber balls with air in them, sponge rubber balls, and homemade string balls. The sponge balls were best for bouncing. The string balls were best for playing baseball, since I did not have a real baseball.

In those days men's work socks were so woven that they could be unraveled into many yards of string. So when socks wore out, we used to unravel them and roll the string into balls. It took a long time to make a string ball, but the finished product was a good ball, suitable for playing catch or baseball. I discovered that if a small, hard rubber ball was used as a core of a string ball, it made a much more lively ball.

Among our most interesting toys were spinning toys. A spinner could easily be made with a large button and a piece of string. The string only had to be laced through the button and tied to form a circle. The button was set spinning, to the delight of any boy and most girls, by holding the string at each end of the circle and pulling and relaxing.

I also made spinning tops from empty thread spools. Making that kind of top required more work than making a button spinner, but it made an excellent toy. All that was needed was a large wooden spool and a short piece of soft lumber.

(Wooden spools were the only kind there were when I was a boy.) Spools that #9 thread came on were the best.

With a sharp knife, I cut from the rim of the spool toward the center. Using slightly more than half of the spool, I trimmed it to a point. Then I made a peg from the soft lumber, just large enough to force through the hole in the spool. I left the short end of the peg protruding about three eights of an inch from the sharp end of the spool and sharpened it to a point. I cut the other end of the peg about three quarters of an inch above the top of the spool. That finished the top. I set it spinning by twisting the peg between my thumb and middle finger and dropping it on a smooth surface. The trick was to see how long I could make the top spin.

Spools were also useful for making other toys. They were nice to roll just as they were, and they were good for making a kind of two-wheeled tractor, using a short stick, a rubber band, and a small piece of soap. There is no need for me to tell how I made the tractors, because no boy in his right mind would bother to make such a toy today. But in my day such toys kept active boys occupied for many happy hours.

Besides homemade balls, marbles, tops, and tractors, I made and flew kites, and I made popguns from elder limbs, stick horses from short sticks, and cars from sticks and small wheels from broken toy wagons that some other child had discarded. I rolled barrel hoops and automobile tires, and I made sleds from scrap lumber so I could go sleigh riding in the wintertime.

I even made rings to wear, molding them from lead, fashioning them with my pocket knife, and plating them with copper. I made a toy boat that was propelled by a rubber band. Add to this the bows and arrows, slings, slingshots, deadfall traps, and fishing tackle I made, and you will begin to see that a boy growing up in the Great Depression was not really poor. In fact, I was exceedingly rich. I had the hills and the valleys to play over, and I had the four seasons of the year to give me variety. I knew instinctively what many have never learned in this affluent day. With the little I had, I knew how to play and how to enjoy life.

In that day people didn't have to be entertained. They entertained themselves. And teenagers didn't need dope to make them high. They were high with the joy of being alive and with the thrill of making the most of what they had.

Even the grown-ups knew how to entertain themselves. Often they got together at night to talk, tell stories, play parlor games and listen to someone play the "banger" and the "gitar."

On Saturdays everybody went to town to sell cream and eggs, and to buy a few groceries, but mostly they went to visit with friends and neighbors. Also on Saturdays, grown-ups sometimes splurged and bought a nickel bottle of pop and a nickel ice cream cone.

I can never forget my grandmother telling

about treating a neighbor woman, who seldom went to town, to her first ice cream cone. When my grandmother had eaten the ice cream off the top and started eating the cone, the lady exclaimed, in some consternation, "Why, Emily, do you eat the box?"

Some people think of "The good old days" as days of hardships. Times were hard, and those of us who lived through them have not forgotten. We had to work hard, and we had little money to buy the things we wanted. Yet, in spite of the hardships, we enjoyed life in a way that people of today cannot understand. Call it nostalgia if you wish, but we often long for the quieter, simpler time we knew in the years gone by.

Chapter 7
The Way Things Used To Be

When I was growing up it was almost as cold in our house in the wintertime as it was outdoors. The only way we could get warm was to huddle around the fireplace and turn ourselves from time to time to warm both our front and back sides. At mealtime we often filled our plates and carried them to our chairs by the fireplace so we could eat with some small degree of comfort.

When we got in bed at night, the sheets were like ice. I spent countless nights shivering on those cold sheets with my knees drawn up toward my chin until the bed finally began to get warm. Then slowly, inch by inch, I moved my toes toward the foot of the bed. On especially cold nights, I used to get under the featherbed and sleep on the straw tick. The cold could not reach me there, so I soon drifted into dreamland.

The next morning about four o'clock, I heard Papa calling, "Louis Walker, get up and build a fire."

I dreaded the cold, and for a moment I lay there debating whether I should dress first or build the fire first. If I built the fire first, the cold would go through my nightclothes as if I were outdoors. If I dressed first, the garments I put on would be like ice to my bare skin.

Our boxed house had been weatherboarded, but there were still cracks in the wall, and the icy wind blew through them with impunity. Often it left a dusting of snow on my bed.

There was no underpinning under our house, and the wind swept under it. There was no sub floor, so the cold easily penetrated the three quarter inch pine floor. Wind even came up through the cracks. When I got out of bed, the linoleum-covered floor was as cold as the ice on the creek.

After I got the fire burning in the grate, I went to the kitchen and started a fire in the cook stove. The water bucket had frozen solid during the night, so I put it on the stove to thaw. Then I went back to the fire I had built in the grate and huddled near it until the room began to warm.

What a blessed day it was when Papa finally bought a Warm Morning heater and put it in the middle bedroom. That big heating stove made the house warmer than it had been since creation, and, when we banked the fire down before going to bed, the house did not get unbearably cold during the night. All I had to do the next morning to get the fire going was to shake out ashes and put in a fresh supply of coal.

In the coming years new inventions that made life easier came along quite often. In my lifetime I have seen changes undreamed of when I was a boy. It has become difficult to remember what life was like without them.

It was a far different world when we did not have central heat, indoor plumbing, a victrola, electric lights, radio, TV, a VCR, or even a phone in our house. I remember when we did not have a washing machine, a refrigerator, or any of the other electrical gadgets we take for granted today.

Somehow in "The good old days," we managed to get along. We did not realize that we were deprived because our neighbors lived the same way we did. We worked hard. We spent hours looking at the Sears and Roebuck, and Montgomery Ward catalogs, and we dreamed of the things we would buy when we got the money.

We had time together as a family, and we had friends, neighbors, and kinfolk who took time to visit us. If they stayed away until we grew lonely for them, we visited them. We had love to spare. We had our dreams, and we took time to play, to fish and to hunt. We had a Bible, and we read it. We had a few good books, among them, *Pilgrim's Progress, The Christian's Secret of a Happy Life,* and a book of Longfellow's poems.

For entertainment, we had a stereoscope and a few pictures for it. I spent many happy hours viewing those pictures over and over. When I was a good-sized boy, we finally bought a second-hand box camera. My what fun we had making pictures with it. Mama managed to buy film, and we made pictures on every occasion. The pictures were black and white, of course, but that did not matter. We thought our camera made better pictures than any other camera in the county.

I will never forget the day a salesman came to our house and convinced Mama to let him demonstrate a new patented washing machine. Anything would have been better than boiling our clothes outside in the double boiler, over an open fire and washing them in a tub with a washboard. So she agreed to let him demonstrate his machine.

Even if we didn't buy it, she reasoned, he would do a week's washing for us, but I would still have to carry water from the creek at the bottom of the hill.

We were so excited at the prospect of seeing how the new washer worked, I carried water and filled all the tubs we had before the salesman arrived. Mama brought out all our dirty clothes and sorted them and put them in separate piles.

When the salesman arrived, we watched him bring in a contraption that looked like anything but a washing machine. Folded up, it stood about as tall as I was, and it was about 30 inches across. It was made of strips of wood that were held together by metal parts. There was a large crank near the top that was attached to some cogs that drove two white rubber rollers.

The man lifted some screen door latches and folded down legs on each side of the contraption. They formed a platform for large washtubs on each side of the upright piece. He brought in two large wooden tubs and a corrugated, wooden roller with some smaller round rollers spring-loaded to it. He set the tubs on the platforms, one on each side, and put the roller assembly in place in one of them. The assembly hooked on the up-right piece and rested in the tub. I know this is complicated, but it is the only way I know to describe the machine.

The salesman had me pour hot water in the tub with the assembly in it. He put in soap and started demonstrating how the machine worked. It was exciting to watch him crank the clothes back and forth through the rollers until they were clean, then crank them through the ringer assembly. That certainly beat ringing clothes by hand.

Mama decided that the machine beat washing the old way all to pieces, so she persuaded Papa to let her buy the machine.

After we got the new machine, it still took a full day for me and Mama to do a week's washing, but it was easier than washing the old way.

Not long after we bought our washing machine, our neighbor bought a new, gasoline-powered model washing machine. They kept it on their back porch so the fumes would not poison them while they were washing. Each time they washed, we could hear the motor of that machine popping as it ran. Perhaps we took comfort that our machine was not as noisy as theirs; it did not make fumes that could poison us, and we did not have to buy gasoline for it.

It was especially exciting when we finally got

a telephone. Several of our neighbors had phones long before we did, and Papa finally broke down and had one installed at our house.

I will never forget the day when two men came to install our phone. Much had already been done to make it possible for us to get a phone, but it still was quite involved to get it installed in our house. Big poles, with many telephone lines, had long since been set along the main roads, and smaller poles, with only two lines, had been set along our road. The big poles, with their strands of wire, added considerably to the scenery along the main roads. I find it nostalgic that they are n gone forever. The present and future generations will never see their like.

Those telephone poles looked like tall crosses with two relatively short crossbars. Each cross-bar had wooden, threaded dowels fastened verti-cally along its top edge, four or five inches apart. A green glass insulator was screwed onto each dowel. Gray uninsulated wires, perhaps #10 gauge, were strung from pole to pole like the strings of great harps. The wires were stretched tight, and, in cold weather, they were said to sing. Many times I have heard the off key, minor hum-ming of the telephone wires.

The poles along our road did not have cross-bars. They had two dowels with green insulators nailed near the top of them. They carried the two lines that made it possible for us to have a phone. The two lines along our road did not sing, but they carried many a conversation.

When the time came for our phone to be installed, they had to set poles across our property to our house. These polls had only one glass insulator to carry a single strand of wire.

I had a natural bent toward all things mechanical or electrical, so when the men came to install our telephone, I watched them with great interest.

One of the men asked Mama where she wanted the phone, and she pointed out a spot near the mantle on our front room wall. The other man went out to their truck and brought in the telephone. It was in a large oak case with a transmitter mounted on an iron extension from the front of the case. There was an oak shelf below that and a pair of round ringers, like the one on top of an alarm clock, mounted near the top. A crank was mounted on the right side of the case, and a hook to hang the receiver on was mounted on the left side. All the metal parts were painted black. The telephone was not pretty by today's standards, but we thought it was a seven day wonder.

One of the men drove a copper rod in the ground near the front step. He connected one of a twisted pair of wires to the ground post and the other one to the telephone line. He ran the twisted wires along the porch ceiling, through the outside wall of the house, and along the wall of the front room to the phone. The other man brought in two large dry cell batteries, put them in the phone case and connected them.

I watched, hardly believing, when he picked up the receiver and turned the crank. The bell on the front of the case rang, and a moment later he started talking to the operator in Lancaster, five miles away.

The man explained to us that we were on a party line with several other families. Each family had a different ring. A single short ring would get one family. Two short rings would get another family. One family's ring was three shorts. Another family's ring was three longs. Besides those rings, there was a short and a long, a long and a short, and so on. Our ring was two longs and a short.

We could call people on our party line by simply ringing their ring with the crank. When we wanted someone who was not on our line, we had to ring the operator in Lancaster. Her ring was a single long ring. When she answered, "Operator," we had to give her the number of the party we wanted. She would plug us into the line we wanted with a patch cord and ring the number we had given her. They left us a small phone book with all the numbers of people in the county.

After the telephone man left, we looked at the phone for a moment. Then Mama looked at the paper she had written the different rings for our neighbors on. She rang the nearest neighbor, and a moment later they were talking. We had really arrived. We had a telephone.

I soon looked inside the phone case and saw that the crank turned an armature inside some large horseshoe magnets. I knew that turning a wire-wound armature inside a magnetic field generated an electric current. So that was what made the phones along the lines ring when the crank was turned, I realized.

I knew that if a person touched a wire that was carrying an electric current it would shock them, so I tried an experiment. I climbed a ladder and tied a piece of copper wire to the telephone wire that ran from our house. Then I climbed down, stood on the moist ground and held the wire, waiting for someone to make a call. Soon somebody did make a call, and I felt my arms tingling and shaking like someone had them in a tight grip and was shaking them. I couldn't decide whether it hurt or tickled. Altogether it was not an unpleasant feeling, and for some days I held to that wire every time I had a chance, waiting to get shocked again. I strongly advise that no one try such an experiment today. The currents we use these days are far too strong to play around with. Touching a live electric wire can be fatal.

I suppose the telephone and the patented washing machine spoiled us. After we got them, we were always wanting something new. When I was in grade school, I remember being made to memorize the phrase, "There is no end to human wants and desires." Alas how true that is. When a person gets something new, they soon want something else.

Material things are nice to have, but they do

not satisfy. Being saved and living right is the only thing that does satisfy. God tells us, ". . . *godliness with contentment is great gain*" (I Tim. 6:6).

All too often we become slaves to the things we have. We often get so many things, it takes all our time to clean, store, and keep them in repair, so we have little time to enjoy them. In the process, we often lose the things that really matter. Our family had had so little for so long, only the shortage of money kept us from buying more than we really needed.

Chapter 8
Work and Relaxation

*P*apa and I worked long and hard to make a living on our little farm. I especially remember chopping weeds out of the cornfield during the hot weather of early July. The corn was over our heads, so not the slightest breeze could reach us. The temperature outside the field was usually in the upper nineties, and, with the hot sun shining down on us, the temperature in the cornfield was well over a hundred. Chopping weeds out of the corn was hard work, and we perspired freely. The sweat bees buzzed around us and often stung us. The ground was dry, and dust fogged up and stuck to our sweat-moistened bodies.

Our days in the fields started early, and it seemed that dinnertime would never come, but we had a way of knowing when it did. A passenger train passed through Lancaster, at 11:30 each morning. The engineer always blew the whistle at the crossing, at the edge of town, and that was our signal that it was dinnertime.

On days when we were plowing with Ol' Jack, one of our work mules, hitched to the double-shovel plow, it was easy to tell when noontime was approaching, even before we heard the train. Ol' Jack apparently had a built in clock, and about fifteen minutes before time for the train, he would start listening for it. With his big ears, he always heard it long before we did, and when the engineer blew the whistle at the crossing, there was no holding him back. He knew we would stop for dinner at the end of the row.

When we were not working Ol' Jack, Papa and I listened for the train. When we heard it, Papa always insisted that we work on to the end of the row before we stopped for dinner, and, like Ol' Jack, I certainly worked fast until we got there.

When we reached the house, Mama always had dinner on the eating table in the kitchen. She too had heard the train and had rushed to have it ready by the time we reached the house.

Mama cooked dinner on our coal-burning stove, and the temperature in the kitchen was even higher than it was in the cornfield. We seldom complained about the heat when we sat down to eat. Mama had worked hard cooking dinner in that hot kitchen, and she was not complaining.

Often Mama dressed and fried a chicken, gathered vegetables from our garden and cooked them, and made biscuits and baked them in the oven. If the ice we had bought in town on Saturday had not all been used or melted, she brewed iced tea. The amber liquid sparkled, and the ice tinkled in the glasses.

We had the luxury of a short rest after dinner. Then we went back to the field and worked until the sun was sinking like an orange ball in the west. That was our signal to leave the field and go to the barn and take the harness off Ol' Jack, if we had worked him. After that we fed the animals, milked the cows, gathered the eggs, and carried in water and coal. Long before we finished, Mama had an oil lamp burning in the kitchen, and we knew that she would soon have supper ready.

We ate supper by the light of the oil lamp in a house that was still as hot as a blast furnace. After supper, I often asked permission to go for a swim in the concrete tank on a neighbor's farm at the foot of our hill. Often my dad went with me. There was no better way to cool off after a hot day in the fields than to take a swim in the tank.

After our swim, we returned to the house and changed clothes. Then Papa and I often went out to the front yard and laid down on the grass. Mama usually sat not far away on the front porch. Lying on our backs, Papa and I looked up at the stars. Usually we started talking, and often we talked about the stars. We wondered how many there were and how far away they were. We often located the Big Dipper, the Little Dipper, and the North Star. Those were the only stars we knew by name.

Sometimes we would see a "falling star," and

we would talk about it. If we saw several in one night, Mama would wonder aloud if that could be a sign. Could it mean that the coming of the Lord was drawing near? We did not know, but it was something to wonder about—and to talk about.

After a while, a cool breeze would fan our bodies. We were tired and sleepy, and the breeze was an invitation to go inside to bed.

We fell asleep with our doors and windows open to let in as much air as possible. In those days, there was almost no crime in our neighborhood, so we did not worry about someone coming in the house to kill or rob us. Our only thought was to get a good night's sleep, because tomorrow would be another hot day, and we would have more work to do.

There were times when work was less pressing, and people had time to sit in swings on their front porches, to rest and to talk. They breathed fresh, country air and felt gentle breezes fan their cheeks, and they watched the real world go by. That beat watching TV by a hundred miles. What people saw from their front porches was real. What people see on TV is make-believe. Even much of the news is contrived, slanted and doctored to fit a particular point-of-view—usually not our point of view. People watch a make-believe world on TV and breathe air that has been cooled by an air conditioner. The only breeze they feel is from an electric fan.

People who have never sat in a swing on a

front porch have no idea what they are missing. While we were sitting on the front porch, old friends sometimes passed in their horse and buggy and waved. We waved back and wondered aloud where they were going, what they would do when they got there, and whom they would see. From time to time, a friend stopped to pass the time of day, and we caught up on the latest neighborhood news, sports and weather.

We would learn that there had been a good rain in the next county, though it was still dry in our locality. We would learn what was in the local paper this week, and what the outcome of the high school football game against a rival team had been last Friday. That kind of sports news meant a lot more than who won a tennis match in England. The report on the weather in the lower end of the county meant a lot more than hearing what the weather was like in Alaska last week. And news of a shooting in the next county last Saturday night meant more than hearing what is happening in Namibia or some other far away place. There was personal news, like how Aunt Susie was faring since her fall and how the new calf that was born last week was doing.

A passerby, who was driving a car, might also pull to the roadside and stop to talk. He might even get out and go with us to see our garden. If he did, we would load him down with summer squash, tomatoes, and cucumbers when he left. Try doing that with the pictures you see on TV. After the visitor was gone, the pastor of the church just might stop by and be invited to sit on the porch with us. When was the last time somebody you saw on TV stopped by for a visit?

After catching up on news about our family and the near neighbors, the pastor just might read to us from the Bible and offer prayer. Then, after being loaded down with fresh eggs and vegetables, he would excuse himself and go on his way, leaving us in a happy frame of mind. If my memory serves me right, it's been a mighty long time since the TV left me feeling like that. No doubt about it, the old front porch was way ahead of TV, and it served us well back when things were the way they used to be.

Of course the front porch was only good for sitting on in the summertime. When cold weather came, our sitting had to be moved to chairs before the fireplace. We gained a lot of comfort when we installed central heating in our homes, but we lost something very valuable. In "The good old days," when the weather was cold, the old-fashioned fireplace brought the family together as they huddled around it to keep warm. Families used to spend countless hours around the fire, and they had time to talk, to share, to play games, to read and to entertain themselves and each other. Being forced to sit close together, they got to know each other better. Neighbors often came to sit with us before the fire, and we got to know them better too. In front of the fire, we exchanged news and discussed problems. Often we shared our burdens. The time around the fireplace made better neighbors.

Just sitting before the fire, even alone, can be an experience not soon forgotten. And it can be a healing experience. King David wrote in Psalm 39:3, *". . . while I was musing the fire burned."* David's heart was hot within him as he sat before the fire. Afterward he cried, *"Lord, make me to know mine end, and measure my days, what it is; that I may know how frail I am."*

In my mind's eye I can still see the smoke curling upward, dancing, white and gray, dying almost away, then rising again. Glowing embers! Amber fire, slowly burning a blackened log. I can still see the sparks fly upward and the flames growing hot when I punched up the fire with a poker.

Who can forget the old family altar before the fireplace? When bedtime drew near, the old family Bible was brought out. The older members of the family became quiet, and the younger ones were made to stop teasing each other and giggling. A chapter was read from the Bible, usually by the father, sometimes by the mother. After that, each member of the family would arise, push their chairs back and kneel before them. Prayers were offered, then good nights were said. After that, by the light of a kerosene lamp, they went to their rooms and to bed.

We lost something when we installed central heating in our homes. Central heating made it possible for family members to scatter all over the house, and the close contact around the fireplace was gone forever. Central heating gave family members more time to themselves and less time for each other.

Television has, to a degree, brought families together again, but it's not the same. Now people sit in their nice, warm family rooms and watch talking pictures on a screen. They no longer entertain each other, nor do they share information with each other. Instead, they listen to news from halfway around the world.

These days it's not even necessary to think or to ask a loved one what they think. The TV people tell us what to think. Of course, there is no time for the family altar these days. Someone might miss the late show. Maybe the people who talk about the good old days have a point after all!

In spite of all the work we had to do in the old days, we still found time for fun and games. Often we got a break on a rainy day. When I was a boy, I welcomed a rainy day, especially in the springtime. A sudden spring rain usually brought a break from work and allowed me time to play.

We had no weather forecast in those days, except what was in *The Farmer's Almanac,* and we didn't fully trust what it said, except when it was time to plant something or to wean a calf. Then we wanted to know if the sign was right.

Rains often came unexpectedly, and we would be caught in the field. When rain began to fall. Papa always insisted that we work on to the end of the row, in the hope that the rain would stop.

Often it would start raining harder, and we would have to drop our hoes where we were and run to the nearest tree for shelter. If the rain did not soon stop, the leaves on the tree would start dripping water, and we would have to run to the barn.

After we got to the barn, Papa would stand near the open door, looking out and wishing the rain would stop. I would look around for a way to entertain myself. Sometimes, if the rain continued, some neighbor boys, wearing raincoats and hats, would come to the barn. One of them would suggest a marble game and bring out a bag of marbles he had in his pocket. We would sweep the dust from a place in the middle of the driveway and draw a ring on the ground for the game. Then we set the marbles in place, chose our taws, and started the game. We passed the time on many a rainy day in this way.

When we had some free time on days when it was not raining, we played horseshoes or baseball. Sometimes the grown-ups joined us in a game of croquet. At night neighbors often got to together for a visit. After we got a victrola, they came more often.

Before we owned an automobile, about all the traveling we did was to town, to the home of my paternal grandparents and to the river to go fishing. All of that we did on horseback or in a buckboard. On Saturday afternoons during the summer, Papa and I often went to Dix River fishing. He did most of the fishing, graveling under rocks for catfish. I mostly just enjoyed playing in the water.

Humorous things sometimes happened when we went fishing. I remember a time when Papa and a neighbor, named Bill, were fishing together in the river. They found a big rock with a large catfish under it, but there was a small problem. The rock was in deep water, and they had to dive to reach the opening under the rock. Papa and ·Bill both wanted to catch that fish, and each was determined to beat the other to it. I have no idea why, but Bill was wearing a large felt hat in the water. He didn't want to get his hat wet, so he took it off and put it on Papa's head. Paying no heed to the hat, Papa dived at the same moment Bill did. As both men disappeared beneath the water, Bill's big hat floated off Papa's head, and the current caught it and carried it down the river. It was really comical to see the hat floating away with neither man in sight.

We used to entertain ourselves by going hunting as well as fishing. We hunted for rabbits, squirrels, and quails. I sometimes hunted for other animals with a .22 rifle. Papa was a good shot with his sawed off, 12 gauge shotgun. I was also a good shot with my rifle, so we usually got our share of game.

Strong in my memory is a hunting trip after I had grown to manhood and moved to my first pastorate. At Thanksgiving, I went home to visit and to go rabbit hunting. One of my deacons and his family went with me. I had been living away from home for a relatively short time, and I was excited that I was going to see Mama and Papa, and that we could put our feet under Mama's table and enjoy the good dinner she was sure to have. I was also excited to have my deacon and his family with me, and, of course, I was excited about going hunting in the old neighborhood. There were always plenty of rabbits on our farm and on adjoining farms, so I assured my deacon that we would have a great day of hunting.

Soon after we arrived, Papa, and my deacon, and I left the house to go hunting. We were glad to be out of doors, and I imagine the women were glad to have us out of the way while they were finishing the Thanksgiving dinner.

When we left the house the sun was shining, and it was so warm it seemed more like early September than late November. But the good weather did not last. We had gone only a short distance when a cold wind started blowing, and clouds started scudding across the sky. We buttoned our coats and continued on our way, expecting no more than a mild change in weather, but we soon learned that a real winter storm was in the making. The temperature plummeted, and snow started falling from the overcast sky.

That day I observed one of the strangest things I have ever seen in nature. We came upon a large snake in the open, almost paralyzed by the cold. It had no business being out that late in the season, and it certainly had no business being out in the weather we were experiencing. It had been so warm in the early part of the day, the snake had crawled from its place of hibernation. The temperature had dropped so suddenly, it had not been able to crawl back.

Never have I seen the weather change more rapidly or more drastically than it did that day. I do not remember killing any rabbits that day, but I do remember that the metal parts of my gun became as cold as ice. My hands ached in spite of the gloves I was wearing.

The wind continued to blow, and the falling snow became so heavy it was difficult to see where we were going, so we decided to give up the hunt and return to the house. On our way we waded the snow and struggled against a blasting wind with an arctic breath. It was difficult to find our way through a slanting wall of white.

Oh how good the house looked when we finally saw it. And it was wonderful to get inside and smell roasting turkey, pungent spices, and a variety of cooking food. Dinner was well under way, and we were glad, for we were hungry after our long walk in the cold.

When dinner was ready, we sat down around the table, now in the dining room, a recent improvement. We enjoyed ham and turkey with dressing and cranberries and a great variety of vegetables, jello, chocolate pudding, and, of course, Mama's specialty, hickory nut cake. What a time we had feasting and visiting. We hardly noticed that the wind was shaking the house, and that the snow was continuing to fall.

Too soon the short winter day was drawing

to a close, and we knew that we should be going home. I opened the door and looked out, and a blast of wind nearly wrenched the door from my hand. I had a glimpse of snow, piled deep and drifted, and I forced the door closed, convinced that the roads were impassable. There was nothing to do but spend the night.

Soon we braved the storm with Papa and helped him feed and milk. The wind had grown colder. Even in the barn the cold was numbing, so we did the chores in record time.

When we finished, we fought our way back to the house, carrying a bucket of milk and some eggs we had gathered. We went out again and carried in water from the cistern and coal from the snow-covered coal pile.

Supper time arrived, and we enjoyed the left-overs. After supper we all crowded around the fireplace in the living room to soak up the heat and to talk. At length bedtime came, and it was good to get in bed and feel the warmth of a feather-erbed. I doubt that I have ever felt more warm and comfortable, but even as I was falling asleep, I worried about the ordeal of going home the next day.

It would be difficult to start the car after it had been in the cold all day and night. After we got it started, we would have to shovel snow away from the wheels. We would probably have to harness the mules and pull the car until we reached the graveled road. Even then, it was possible that the car would get stuck in the snow, and we would have to jack up the back wheels, one at a time, and get down on our knees in the snow and put chains on the tires.

I do not remember the details or the trials of the journey home. It was likely the way I had envisioned it while lying there in the featherbed.

My father and mother have long been gone to Heaven, so I can no longer visit them, but I am glad that I can relive in memory that snow-filled Thanksgiving Day of long ago. It is one of those special, treasured memories.

Chapter 9

My Most Embarrassing Moments

I grew up at the end of the road and the head of the creek. My parents were timid, and I grew up as timid as they were. It is likely that the isolation of our home also contributed to my timidity.

I had little contact with other children until we moved to the farm where I grew up. I was six when we moved, and I was delighted that our nearest neighbor, a quarter mile away, had a little girl about my age. I played with her occasionally. Within a year or two, her family moved away, and a new family moved in the house they had vacated. They had a large family, and some of their boys were about my age. I played with them when I could, but my contact with them did not get me over my timidity. Being timid and self-conscious caused me to commit some embarrassing blunders in my early life.

About the time I was old enough to begin to be attracted to girls, I visited in the home of a friend who had two or three sisters. Some other young people were there visiting also. In the afternoon, we all wandered into the bedroom of the parents and sat down on the edge of the bed to look at some pictures.

Shortly one of the boys poked me in the ribs. I jumped and landed back on the bed. There was a loud cracking sound, as the bed rail split from end to end, and the bed crashed to the floor. I was so mortified, I left at once. I doubt that I ever set foot in that house again.

Another most embarrassing moment occurred in the home of the barber, who cut my hair for the going price of 35 cents. We became friends, and one afternoon after he closed his shop, he invited me to his home.

When I arrived, he introduced me to his wife, an attractive, neatly dressed, apparently well educated young woman. I was ill-at-ease from the moment I saw her.

She soon brought out some berries and cream and maybe some cookies, and put them on a small table. Then she invited me and her husband to come to the table and partake of her refreshments. Despite my timidity, I managed to eat my bowl of berries and the cookies without mishap. Then I made a most embarrassing blunder.

At home I had developed a bad habit. No one told me it was a bad habit, so I continued to do it until it became second nature. Where I ate at the table, my chair was near the wall, and I had a habit of tilting my chair against the wall after I finished eating. So, when I finished eating my bowl of berries, I tilted my chair back as I always did at home. But there was no wall behind me. So my chair kept going, and on its way down, it struck a floor lamp and knocked it over. The power cord tangled around my arm. My feet went up under the tabletop, and the table started rising like a hot-air balloon.

Dishes rattled and started sliding across the table. I knew that everything on the table was going to crash to the floor, that the pretty china was going to be broken, and that cream and berry juice were going to spill all over the expensive rug. But the barber saved the day. He instantly put both hands on top of the table and pressed down. That kept the table from upsetting, but it didn't keep me from landing on the floor.

Embarrassed beyond words, I crawled from under the table, disentangled the electric cord from around my arm, and set the floor lamp upright. My friend's quick action saved the china, but it did nothing for my bruised feelings. I soon excused myself and left. He never invited me back.

I will never forget the day I almost lost my sermon. During the first summer of my ministry, I was holding a meeting in a one-roomed schoolhouse, in a community where there was no church. In this school, as in other schools in that day, the teacher taught several grades in one room. There were children of all ages and sizes, so they had desks of varying sizes. The largest desks were in the back of the room and the smallest in the front, near the teacher's desk.

I was a young, single preacher, and many young people attended the meeting. Some of the girls sat near the front, so they would be near the preacher, I suppose. A young lady, who was large for her age, and decidedly overweight, came down front and sat at a tiny desk that was designed for a child in the first grade. The desks in those days were made with the desk top fastened to the back of the seat. The desk in front of a pupil was part of the next seat. These desks were fastened to the floor with not much room between the seat and the desk top in front of it. I hope you get the idea.

Well, this large girl came down the aisle to one of these tiny seats and poured herself into it. She filled all the space between it and the desk top in front of her. She overflowed all around the seat. It looked as if the seat was not there, and the desk top was smothered under her big arms.

I paid no attention to her or the seat until she got amused, no tickled is the word, at something I said. I have no memory of what I said that tickled her, but I have never forgotten how she reacted. She turned her head back and opened her mouth wide enough to swallow a large biscuit without chewing. She laughed until the windows rattled, and she beat on the little desk with her big hands until the poor thing creaked and quivered and groaned. I though she would break it into splinters. I got tickled at her, and I laughed.

Everyone else was laughing, and there was no way to stop them.

I tried to go on with my sermon. I turned my eyes toward the ceiling so I would no longer see the girl, but I could not forget her. Every time I opened my mouth to say something, I broke out laughing again. I doubt that the service that day did anything for anyone else, but it did a lot for me. It taught me the value of having my emotions under control, no matter what happens.

Another most embarrassing event occurred soon after I became pastor of two half-time churches, Mitchellsburg Baptist Church in Mitchellsburg, Kentucky, and Salem Baptist Church, three miles over the knob from Mitchellsburg. This was my first experience as a pastor, and I was just a timid, inexperienced country boy. I had a lot to learn, and I needed the rough edges knocked off of me. The Lord knew how to knock those rough edges off, and I think He let some things happen just for that reason.

Salem Baptist Church had a typical, one-roomed, frame church building. There was only one door to get in or out of the building. All the Sunday school classes met in that one room without even curtains to separate them. There was no plumbing and no electricity. So there were no electric lights. Air-conditioning had not been invented, and furnace heat was rare. So Salem Baptist Church was hot in the summertime and cold in the winter. In summer the people tried to cool themselves with hand-held fans the undertaker had given the church so that if any of them died, they would know who to call. In the winter the people huddled around the potbellied stove near the center of the building.

At night, summer or winter, they squinted at songbooks by the light of coal oil (kerosene) lamps that were mounted along the walls. Shinny reflectors behind the lamps made them give a little more light, but they still did a poor job of lighting the building.

The people at Salem loved the Lord, and perhaps they were as excited to have me for their pastor as I was to be their pastor. But they could not have been as ill-at-ease as I was.

The first Sunday night I preached for them, it troubled me that the church was so poorly lighted. The new Aladdin kerosene lamps had come on the market not long before that. I thought the Aladdin Lamp was the greatest thing since the invention of the wheel. That lamp brought better light to country people who did not have electricity. It was the greatest improvement in oil lamps since the time of Abraham. In his day, and in the days when Jesus was on earth, an oil lamp was a small container of oil with a wick. The first improvement on the oil lamps was when someone figured out how to put a glass chimney over the flame. That was the kind of lights we used when I was a boy. Then came the marvelous Aladdin Lamp, with a mantle that contained the flame so that it made the mantle glow. That kind of lamp was much brighter than the old-fashioned lamps. I decided right away that Salem Baptist Church had to have an Aladdin Lamp.

I never thought to ask the church to buy a lamp. Instead, I bought one out of my meager funds. The Aladdin Lamp I bought had a chain so it could be hung from the ceiling.

The next Sunday that I preached at Salem, I proudly gave the lamp to the church. The men of the church hung it that afternoon. That night there was light in the old church building such as had never been before.

I only preached at Salem every other Sunday, so before I returned to preach again, the oil in the lamp had to be replenished. Whoever put the oil in the lamp must have decided that the glass shade wasn't worth the trouble it took to remove it and replace it each time they filled the lamp with oil. So, instead of putting it back on the lamp, they placed it in the middle of the bench behind the pulpit.

On my next appointed Sunday, I returned to Salem to preach, officiate might be a better word. I was all the staff the church had, so I had to lead the singing, make the announcements, call for the deacons to receive the offering, pray over it, and preach. Now remember that I was inexperienced and that I was half scared to death when I was in the pulpit. In those days, I didn't know what to do with my hands when I was in the pulpit or what to do with the rest of me for that matter. I sometimes stood behind the pulpit desk.

Often I moved from side to side, or walked back and forth across the platform. Sometimes, for no reason at all, I sat down on the bench behind the pulpit stand.

That Sunday, about the middle of the third song, I backed up and sat down on the glass shade that was in the middle of the bench. You talk about pandemonium! The shade didn't crash. It exploded! I jumped straight up in the air and landed in the midst of the glass that had scattered all over the pulpit. The day was ruined for me. I was embarrassed and humiliated beyond words. I couldn't walk for the glass on the floor, so for once I stood in one place and preached. How I ever got through that sermon, I'll never know.

I'm sure the people did not soon forget what happened that day, and I have certainly never forgotten it. The memory now brings me a smile, but it was no laughing matter when it happened. I'm sure that this experience, and others like it, helped to prepare me for hard knocks I would have later in my ministry.

The time came when an embarrassing situation troubled other people more than it did me, for I had learned to shrug off such events and go on as though they had not happened.

After I had become well known as a radio preacher, I was invited to hold a revival in a good-sized country church near Berea, Kentucky. The church did not have a pastor at the time, so the deacons were in charge. They must have thought

I was a big-shot preacher, for they were on pins and needles. They had everything planned down to a T. They wanted everything to be in order. They received an offering every night, and they gave it to me in cash, just as it came in. I think they must have agreed how much each person would give each night, for the offering was always the same amount. Just an example of how they wanted things to go.

Above the pulpit desk in that church, there was a hanging lamp of ancient vintage. It had once been an oil-burning lamp, but it had been electrified. It was a curious looking lamp, with a clear bowel for oil, and with two burners, with glass chimneys, going off at 45 degree angles. The bowl was filled with a good quantity of water, I suppose to make it look as if it had oil in it. Now, that lamp must have been hanging there since the flood, but when they introduced me, and I stepped forward and laid my open Bible on the desk, that thing fell. It struck the desk just above my Bible. It broke! It wet my Bible, and it nearly drowned me. And shattered glass went everywhere.

Women rushed to the pulpit and started mopping up the water with a tablecloth, or something they had miraculously gotten from somewhere. Men came and started picking up pieces of glass as if they were collecting diamonds. Somebody blotted the water off my Bible, and someone tried to brush the water off the front of my coat, tie, and shirt.

I told the people it was all right, that I suppose that lamp had to fall sometime, and now was as good a time as any. Really, I don't remember all I said, but I shrugged it off and went on with the service. By that time I was casehardened to such incidents, but the people of that church were not. They were so mortified, I doubt that they heard anything I said that night.

Chapter 10
Molding Influences

*M*y mother carried me to the church across the road from where I was born when I was a baby. She wanted to make sure nothing was lacking in my upbringing, but it was not always possible for her to keep me in church.

My father soon gave up blacksmithing and moved to a farm on a back road, too far from a church for Mama to attend. A year or two later, we moved again. This time we settled on a good road, but again there was no church nearby. Having no way to travel except on horseback, Mama did not attend church while we lived there. Our next move was to a farm on the County Pike, in Garrard County, where I grew up. Again, there was no church near enough for Mama to attend, but there was a summertime Sunday school on Sunday afternoons at Hyattsville, two miles from where we lived. She took me there to Sunday school. That was my first memory of attending any kind of religious service. I was so small my feet did not touch the floor when I sat on the homemade pews.

I recall little of what I was taught in Sunday school, but I remember the beautiful cards they passed out each Sunday. I treasured them even more than the bird pictures I got out of Arm & Hammer baking soda boxes. I got one bird picture each time my mother opened a box. We must have used a lot of soda, for I accumulated quite a number of those pictures.

The Sunday school cards were not as pretty as the bird pictures, but they had words on the back, and Mama used to read them to me after we got home.

When I was about nine or ten years old, a preacher and a singer came to our neighborhood and got permission to hold a revival in the Sunday school building. They stayed at our house, and we rode to church with them every night in the preacher's car. Mama and Papa agreed that the preacher couldn't preach much, but they thought the singer was all right.

I remember hearing the preacher and the singer practice singing at our house. One of their songs was *No Disappointment In Heaven.* I had never heard it before, and I thought it was beautiful. The meeting lasted two weeks, and I was the only one converted. That put me in good company. Dr. B. R. Lakin and Dr. George Truett were the only converts in revivals they attended when they were boys.

I'm not sure the preaching had any effect on me, but one night during the invitation, a neighbor lady asked me if I didn't want to be saved. I told her I didn't know. She whispered that my mother was praying for me. I looked and saw that my mother's lips were moving in prayer. That was all it took. I went forward and knelt at an old wooden bench at the front of the building and received Jesus as my Savior.

I slept that night with a new peace in my heart, and the next morning, as I walked the graveled road to school, I felt as if I were walking on air. As I drew near the country schoolhouse where I went to school, someone shouted, "Hello, sanctified." That was my first taste of persecution. It made my heart ache, but it did not keep me from being glad I was a Christian.

For a time I was the only Christian in my school, but the school was not entirely without Christian influence. We always sang a song or two before starting our lessons. The teacher always read a passage from the Bible and had us to recite the Lord's Prayer. How sad that teachers are not allowed to do that in our schools today.

Our family was faithful in church attendance for a year or two after I was saved, and those were the happiest days of my boyhood. With pleasure, I remember putting my 5 cent offering (contributed by my parents) in an envelope and placing it in the collection plate each Sunday morning. I loved my pastor, and to this day I treasure a hug he gave me at the door one Sunday morning as I was leaving the church. How easy it was for him to give me that precious memory!

Not long after I was converted, my parents took me to a revival meeting at the courthouse in Lancaster. I do not remember the preacher's name, but I recall that his family played several musical instruments and that great crowds attended the meeting. That meeting made a profound impression on me.

We attended another revival, held in a crowd-packed tobacco warehouse that had been refurbished and seated for the meeting. We attended several meetings in gospel tents after that. Though I was but a boy, I listened attentively to the sermons in all those meetings. I remember none of the texts or outlines, but I do remember many of the illustrations the preachers used. From those preachers I learned the value of a good story well told. The earnestness of those revival preachers, the invitations they extended, and the people who went forward made impressions that remains with me to this day.

From the time I was saved I felt the call to preach, and I soon told some of my schoolmates that God had called me to preach. I did not own a Bible, but I found a ragged piece of a Bible that someone had discarded. I started reading and studying it, and one afternoon, on the way home from school, I announced to those who were walking with me that I was going to preach them a sermon. I started preaching, and I preached by the mile instead of the clock. I ended my sermon when I turned on the drive that lead up the hill to my house. I promised to preach them another one the next morning. I believe I would have preached from that day, if someone had helped me get started.

In my teen years, our family stopped attending church. Not long afterward I drifted away from the Lord and gave up the idea of preaching. I did not think of preaching again until our family returned to church, and I rededicated my life to the Lord. By that time I did not want to preach, but every time I prayed, I knew the Lord was calling me. I made excuses, but the Lord showed me they were not reasons.

One morning about that time, Papa sent me to the back of the pasture to bring up the cows. It was a beautiful, warm morning. The grass was wet with dew, and the morning sun was turning every dewdrop into a diamond. Morning glories were in bloom along the fence rows. The due-wet grass came halfway to my knees. A field-lark, startled by my tread, sprang into the sky with plaintive cry.

I had an awesome sense of the presence of God. His hand was upon me, and I knew He was calling me to preach. I prayed aloud as I walked. My prayer was something like this: "Dear Lord, I don't know how to preach. I don't know how to prepare a sermon. I don't have a voice suitable for preaching, but I believe you are calling me. If You'll give me the voice I need, and if You'll teach me what I need to know, and if You'll give me open doors and people to preach to, I'll preach for You the best I can."

I know the Lord heard my prayer. In time I learned how to prepare sermons and preach them. Doors opened to me, and people came to hear me preach. The Lord also did something for my voice. Often I have preached five or more times a day, for months at a time, and my voice has been adequate for the task. It is still serving me well.

Not long after that morning talk with the Lord, I told my pastor the Lord had called me to preach. The church soon licensed me to preach, and the following Wednesday night I preached my first sermon. I was scared to death, almost, but I managed to get through a short message. Afterward, my critical English teacher complimented me. From that day until this, I have followed the gospel trail wherever it has led me, and God has blessed and used me.

Since I have been in the ministry, some of God's great preachers have greatly influenced my life. One of them was Mordicia Ham. Dr. Ham started preaching about the turn of the century, but it was not until 1913 that he had a meeting that resulted in a thousand professions. The 1930s were the most fruitful years of Dr. Ham's ministry. During that period he often had meetings that resulted in thousands of conversions.

I first heard of Dr. Ham in the late 1930s, when he held a meeting in Lexington, Kentucky, about forty miles from my home. During that meeting, he broadcast a daily service over radio station WLAP, one of the three stations we could get on our battery-powered radio. We could not go to Lexington to attend the meeting, but we listened to Dr. Ham on radio every day.

From the first broadcast, I realized that there was something unique about Dr. Ham's preaching. His voice was clear and slightly high pitched. He spoke almost in a monotone. At times he seemed to hesitate and hang on a word for emphasis. He had the ability to project his personality through the loud speaker of the radio, and the effect was captivating.

As Dr. Ham preached, he drew from his memory passages from the Bible to drive home the point he was making. The preaching of Dr. Ham and the singing of Mr. Vick, his associate, soon became the chief topic of conversation everywhere the radio station was heard.

Dr. Ham was the first evangelist of national reputation I had ever heard, even on the radio. Some years later I heard him in person at Frankfort, Kentucky. I cannot describe how thrilled I was to sit in the crowded auditorium and hear him preach.

Even now I can see him in my mind's eye as he stood in the pulpit. He was tall, large of frame, but not overweight. His dark eyes, looking through rimless glasses, seemed to burn into my soul. Lines between his eyes made him appear intense. He wore a well-trimed mustache, and from time to time his lips threatened to smile, so he did not appear severe. He was dressed in a conservative dark suit, and he looked more like a lawyer than he did a preacher.

In person, he sounded much as he did on radio, and his voice and message held me spellbound. Little did I dream that in time I would come to know Dr. Ham, that we would become good friends, and that he would take the liberty of calling to invite himself to preach in my pulpit. In my wildest imagination, I never dreamed that he would one day give me a daily broadcast he had built up on a 50 thousand watt radio station in Corpus Christi, Texas.

Dr. Ham told me of some of his great meetings. In the days when meetings were held in tabernacles that were especially built for them, he preached every night, except Monday night, for months at a time. In Nashville, Tennessee, in a meeting that lasted eight months, eight thousand people were baptized into the membership of the cooperating churches.

The following has nothing to do with how Dr. Ham influenced my life, but it does have to do with something God used to build my faith.

One Monday morning, Dr. Ham phoned me from his home in Louisville and told me that he was coming to Lexington the next day on business. Could I meet him at the airport? I assured him that I would be happy to meet him. His plane was to arrive shortly before noon, so I invited him to go to lunch with me. He gladly accepted, and I told him I would be waiting at the airport when his plane arrived.

Later that day, some unexpected expense took all the money I had. I could have borrowed the money for lunch for myself and Dr. Ham, but I decided that I would ask the Lord for daily bread instead.

Though I tried to leave the need in the Lord's hands, the next morning I started trying to figure out how the Lord would supply my need. On rare occasions in the past, someone had sent me a personal gift in the mail. I decided that was what would happen today. So I went to the post office early, picked up the mail, hurried to my office, and opened it. To my dismay, there was no offering for me.

Our church had just finished building a new auditorium, and often friends would come to watch my ten o'clock broadcast and to see the new building. Sometimes they would hand me a personal offering before leaving. I decided that was what would happen today, but no one came to watch the broadcast. When the broadcast was over, I decided that whoever was coming must be running late. So I waited for them to come as long as I could before leaving for the airport. No one showed up in the allotted time, so, somewhat distressed, I left for the airport.

On the way to the airport, I was still trying to figure out how the Lord was going to give me and Dr. Ham our daily bread. I decided that I would see someone at the airport who would hand me some money, but at the airport, the only person I saw that I recognized was a policeman, and he did not offer to give me anything.

Dr. Ham's plane arrived, and he got off. My pressure was building as he came through the gate. I greeted him and led him to my parked automobile. We got in, and I started driving toward Lexington.

Dr. Ham was in a good mood, and he talked all the way. He didn't know it, but he was interrupting my praying. It wasn't easy to keep up with his conversation and talk to the Lord at the same time. I confess that I did more praying than listening to Dr. Ham.

I still believed that the Lord was going to meet my need, but I thought He might need a little help. So I decided what I should do.

"Dr. Ham, it's a beautiful day. Would you mind walking a short distance on our way to the restaurant?" I asked.

"I would enjoy the walk," he replied.

So I parked my car a good two blocks from a restaurant on Main Street. I thought that surely, if we walked that far, we would meet someone I knew, and they would hand me some money. Dr. Ham walked slowly, and I did not hurry him. Even so that was the shortest two blocks I ever walked, and I did not see anyone I knew on the way.

We reached the restaurant, went in, and found ourselves a table. Dr. Ham was still talking, and I was still praying. I found myself hoping that he was not hungry, though that really would not have made any difference. I didn't have enough money to pay for a hamburger.

Dr. Ham must have been hungry, for he ordered a full meal. I decided if I was going to have to wash dishes for our food, I might as well wash a lot of them, so I also ordered a full meal.

While we were waiting for the waitress to bring our food, Dr. Ham continued to talk, and I continued to pray. Soon the waitress brought the food, and I asked Dr. Ham to thank the Lord. While he did, I kept praying for a miracle.

Just as Dr. Ham finished praying, a man I did not recognize came to our table and handed me some bills.

"Brother Arnold, I want to pay for your dinner," he said.

I thanked him, and in my heart, I thanked the Lord.

When we finished eating, I paid the check, left a tip for the waitress and walked out of the restaurant with some jingling money in my pocket.

I never told Dr. Ham that I could not have paid for our meal without the donation. It was one of those things that was just between me and the Lord.

There came a time when I left my pastorate in Lexington to do mission and revival work. Some months later, I was back in Kentucky and learned that Dr. Ham was seriously ill. I went to his home in Eminence, Kentucky to see him. He was bedfast and nearing the crossing of the river.

We talked and reminisced for a time. When it

was time for me to go, we prayed together. Then I bade my old friend good-bye. I never saw him again, but I will see him on the other side of the river. I'm glad our paths crossed.

When I was growing up, I often heard of Gypsy Smith. In that day, even in rural America, the famed English evangelist's name was a household word. Gypsy Smith was born in a Gypsy tent in England. When he was converted, at the age of 19, he could not read or write. Yet he became a mighty evangelist.

In the early years of my ministry, I was greatly excited when I learned that Gyspy Smith was to hold a revival in Huntington, West Virginia, not far from where I was pastoring. I decided at once that I would attend every service possible.

I arrived early at the opening service, so I would be sure to get a seat. People were already arriving, and they continued to arrive until the great auditorium and the horseshoe balcony were packed. I could scarcely contain my excitement when the evangelist appeared on the platform. He was eighty-four years old, but he appeared to be no more than fifty. He was short and stocky, and he moved quickly, giving the appearance of great reserves of energy. His hair was iron gray, his complexion a bit dark, and his face was almost without lines or wrinkles.

Gypsy Smith moved quickly to the front of the platform, and, without a glance at the great, expectant audience, he knelt, laid his arm on the railing and bowed his head in silent prayer. A holy hush settled upon the audience while he prayed. I felt constrained to join him in silent prayer.

When Gypsy finished praying, he walked straight to the podium, picked up a songbook and announced the opening hymn. He led his own singing in a remarkably clear, strong soprano voice. He often stopped to read a verse, and as he read, the familiar words took on new meaning. Then, as Gypsy led the congregation in singing the verse he had just read, I found myself joining in with all my heart.

At length the evangelist laid down his songbook and picked up his Bible and read from it in a conversational tone, as he had from the hymnbook. He preached in the same way, and while he was preaching, time seemed suspended. The multitude was caught up in his words. A spiritual atmosphere pervaded the place, and people seemed almost not to breathe as they listened.

The message ended all too soon, though the speaker had been speaking for almost an hour. Then he started giving an unusual invitation. It seemed almost that he was afraid to invite people to come forward, less someone be injured in the crush of those that would respond.

When he did make his appeal, great numbers responded at once. He asked those who would receive Christ as Saviour to stand, and hundreds stood up all over the great auditorium and in the balcony. The evangelist dealt with them as if he were dealing with one person. He seemed to be talking to each one individually as he explained to them how to receive Christ as Savior. Then he had them indicate that they had trusted the Lord with an upraised hand, and the ushers started passing cards to them so they could record their decisions. The cards were later passed on to co-operating pastors so they could follow up those who had responded. Never have I seen a man who was so used to deepen the spiritual lives of Christians and to bring the lost to Christ.

It is difficult to explain how Gypsy Smith touched my life. He reminded me of an Old Testament prophet. His ministry deepened my spiritual life and added a new dimension to my ministry.

Chapter 11
My Fascination With Radio and Recorders

*R*adio broadcasting has long been a major part of my ministry, and it still is. I have preached to many thousands by radio. Many have been converted through this ministry. Untold numbers have been brought closer to the Lord, and preachers and missionaries have been called into the ministry.

I was a boy the first time I saw and heard a radio. One day in Lancaster, my mother and I heard loud music coming from an open window of an office above the First National Bank. Someone told us it was coming from a radio. We had never heard of a radio, so we decided to go upstairs to the office and investigate. When we reached the office, we were allowed to go in and see the new contraption.

The radio covered a large table. It had a large, S shaped horn rising above it, and it had enough wires running from it to wire a small city. Tangled wires were all over the tabletop. They hung over the sides of the table, and there were more wires under the table.

The looks of the contraption did not trouble us, but we were greatly puzzled that it was playing music loud enough to fill the room and spill out the window into the town below. We had no idea where the music was coming from.

Someone told us that the music was coming through the air from a distant city. That we could hardly believe. To us it seemed impossible that music could come through the air. There had to be some trick, though we had no idea what it was. We were so filled with amazement we talked about the radio all the way home and for many days to come. Finally we learned that the radio really had been invented, and that, by some miracle we did not understand, it could catch sounds that were produced many miles away. Right then we decided that someday we had to have a radio.

Some years later, after I had become a teenager, we did buy a radio. The used radio we bought was in a small wood case designed to set on a tabletop. It had only two vacuum tubes, and it was battery powered. Instead of a speaker, then called a horn, it had two sets of headphones. Only two people could listen to it at a time, but oh how we enjoyed that radio. Sometimes we took one of the phones off the head bracket so Papa, Mama and I could all listen at the same time.

I soon learned that a long, high antenna and a good ground would enable the radio to bring in many more stations. So I strung a piece of antenna wire between the top of the house and the top of the barn. After that it was great sport to tune in stations from distant cities. We kept a list of the stations we tuned in and tried to get them again. We soon learned that we could not get the same stations every night.

Often we were up late at night listening, and I almost always turned on the radio each morning as soon as I finished my early morning chores. Most programs had live performers in those days, and I found a powerful station in Del Rio, Texas, that had a musician on at 4:00 a.m. that I really liked. After that, I missed very few mornings tuning in that station.

In time we got a better radio, complete with A batteries, B batteries, and a C battery. It also had a loud speaker. With great excitement, I figured out how to hook the radio to the batteries and to the antenna and ground wires. Then we turned it on and thrilled at all the things that came out of the speaker.

We soon found some special programs we listened to every day. At night we listened to Lowell Thomas and the news, and we listened to Kate Smith sing, *God Bless America.* I doubt that Lowell Thomas has ever been equaled as a newscaster. He told it like it was without telling us what we were supposed to think about it. Few singers have influenced a generation of Americans as Kate Smith did.

Early each morning we tuned in *The Nation's Family Prayer Period,* broadcast over WLW in Cincinnati, from Cadle Tabernacle in Indianapolis. E. Howard Cadle was pastor of the tabernacle and speaker on the broadcast. Mrs. Cadle warmed our hearts each morning by singing the theme, *Ere you left your room this morning, did you think to pray?* After another song, Buford Cadle presented his father, and he preached a homespun sermon with compassion and power. Few, if any, radio broadcasts preached the gospel to as many at that time as *The Nation's Family Prayer Period* did.

We listened to Dr. B. R. Lakin, after he came to the tabernacle as co-pastor and later as pastor. I became acquainted with Dr. Lakin while he was at the tabernacle. Little did I dream at the time that one day we would become good friends and that I would follow him on the radio program he founded.

After I answered the call to preach, I knew right away that I wanted to preach on radio. My first radio broadcast was over a small, home-built, bootleg radio station that was on the air for two or three hours each Sunday morning. Much later, after I became pastor of a church in East Kentucky, I drove more than a hundred miles to speak on a program that was conducted by a preacher I knew. In time I started a radio ministry. I have been on radio daily, without interruption, since 1947. I believe my broadcast is the longest running daily broadcast, conducted by the same preacher, in history.

Dr. B. R. Lakin started his own network program, *The Voice of the Appalachians,* after he left

Cadle Tabernacle. In his later years, because of failing health, he gave me the program. I still preach on that program, and I still hear from some of the people who used to hear Dr. Lakin, and, before him, Mr. Cadle. I continued my daily radio ministry, called *Preaching at Your House,* after taking over Dr. Lakin's program.

Recorders of one sort or another have long been a vital part of radio broadcasting, and I have used many of them. From the time I was a teenager, I was interested in recording machines. I have watched them evolve from crude mechanical recorders to the sophisticated recorders we have today.

In a recent church service, I was impressed by the superb sound track being played from a cassette tape to accompany some special singers. That started me thinking about the stages in the development of the recorders that are now so much a part of our lives. The following is a bit of the history of the evolution of the records we use today.

In 1877, Thomas A. Edison invented the first sound recorder. It was a primitive contraption with a cylinder made of wax and tinfoil. To test the machine, Edison had one of his assistants turn the cylinder with a crank while he shouted the nursery rhyme *Mary Had a Little Lamb* into a horn. At the small end of the horn was a diaphragm with a needle attached to it. The needle cut a vibrating track in the tinfoil. The sound played back when the needle was again made to run in the grove. That was the first recording in history.

In time Edison came out with a phonograph, with recordings made on wax cylinders. A large morning-glory shaped horn amplified the sound mechanically. A later model of Edison's phonograph had a turntable that played a recording from a thick disk. Several other companies soon produced phonographs, similar in design but not compatible with the Edison machine. The phonograph has been called by many names, such as, the gramophone, the victrola, the record player, and the stereo.

The first major improvement in these machines was the introduction of electronically recorded sound. The sound was further enhanced when played back on an electronic record player.

For a number of years recordings were pressed on shellac disk that played back at 78 RPM. The shellac recordings were eventually replaced by vinyl disk that were less scratchy, and had better sound quality. Not long after that, the industry came out with 45 RPM singles and 33 and 1/3 RPM albums. Stereo sound soon followed, and the recording industry continued to grow.

People now enjoy the best sound ever put on records, but I have never enjoyed any records as much as I did the ones we played on the victrola Mama ordered from Sears and Roebuck when I was a boy. Some of our neighbors had better victrolas long before we got ours, but they could not have enjoyed theirs any more than we did ours. Often I had gone to listen to their records on their victorlas, but it was different after we got our own and could start building a library of our own records and could have the neighbors come to our house to hear them.

In my teen years, after I had learned to play a guitar and sing, I used to look at crude recorders in the Sears and Roebuck catalog, consisting of a turntable, a tin horn and a cutting needle, and wish I had the money to buy one. I even tried to make one. It was not a success. Little did I dream that the time would come when most teenagers would have very satisfactory recorders that cost only a few dollars.

Early in my radio ministry I found it necessary to record some of my broadcast. In the beginning the recorders I used cut groves in acetate disks and recorded sound on them in one pass. They were far from satisfactory, so other means of recording were invented. As far as I know, the earliest of these was the wire recorder. It was soon replaced by the tape recorder. Next came the cassette recorder, and soon many Americans were carrying small cassette recorders around with them and making their own recordings.

The early tape recordings used 1/4 inch tape. They were bulky and heavy, and the quality of recordings made on them was not good. Later models did make good recordings, and they became the standard for radio broadcasting.

When the cassette recorder came along, with its smaller tape and slower speed, it was not considered good enough to use for serious broadcasting, but soon the dolby enhancement and other refinements improved the quality. Now most radio stations use cassette recorders, and more music cassettes are sold today than any other kind of recordings, including the exceptionably good CDs. Soon we are to have digital cassette recording that will equal the sound quality of CDs. No one knows what will come next.

There is not room to write at length of sound recorded on film, made by a light beam, or recording on computers, using tape, disk, CD-ROM, the worm system, and some others.

In my early ministry, I recorded sermons for radio broadcast on acetate disk. The sound was fair, but the disks were often spoiled in the recording process and had to be made over. A further problem was that a 16 inch disk would only hold 15 minutes of recording. A 30 minute broadcast required two disks. When the first disk ran out of space, I had to pause in my sermon, then start again at the same place on the second disk. I used to record several of theses every week and ship them off to radio stations.

At the radio station, the operator had to use two turntables and cue one disk on each turntable. He had to switch from one turntable to the other in the middle of the sermon. Also, he had to listen carefully, lest the playback needle hang in one of the grooves and start playing the same phrase over and over again.

I used a wire recorder to record my sermons when they first came out, but the sound was poor, and the fine wire often broke. If that happened while the program was on the air, the sermon stopped until the operator tied a knot in the wire and started the recorder playing again. It is no wonder that wire recorders soon passed off the scene.

When the 1/4 inch tape recorder came out, I bought one to use for our broadcasts. Even with its poor quality, it was better than a disk recorder. Soon a better model tape recorder came out, and the broadcast industry switched to it. I bought one of the better machines, and my ministry of broadcasting on tape really was under way.

Those recorders were not stereo, but they were good. I used that kind of recorder long after stereo came out and long after radio stations had switched to cassette tape. A lightning strike on the electric line finally finished most of our old equipment, and we were forced to upgrade. Now our programs are recorded on broadcast quality stereo cassette recorders.

A radio ministry is not easy. A schedule of broadcasting must be met. A fresh message is needed every day. Contracts must be made with radio stations, funds raised and bills paid. In the years gone by, I used to record broadcasts long into the night before leaving for meetings. I now have it a bit more organized, but I still have to make recordings ahead of time each time I am going to be away.

My busy schedule of revivals, radio broadcast and writing continues. I broadcast on the radio every day, and I have a weekly broadcast that is aired on several stations every week. I publish *The Arnold Report* every month, and I normally preach in more than thirty churches each year. I travel thousands of miles to get to these churches. I write every day, unless I am driving to or from meetings in my car. I also operate a mail order business to distribute the books I have written and good books by other authors. The work is tiring, but I am not looking for a rocking chair. A fire was kindled in my soul early in life, and it has not gone out. I pray that it never will.

I thank God for radio stations and for recorders. They have served me well for many years. Man's ability to record both sound and pictures brings to mind the fact that God was recording long before man ever thought of recording either sound or pictures. There are several verses in the Bible that tell us of God making a record of all that we say and do. There is a most interesting verse in Psalm 87:6. *"The LORD shall count, when he writeth up the people, that this man was born there."* This indicates that God makes a record of each person's life, even including his birthplace. In the Gospels of Matthew and Luke (Matthew 10:30; Luke 12:7), we are told that the hairs of our heads are numbered, and in Ecclesiastes 12:14 that God will bring every secret thing to judgment. In Revelation 20 we are told that the books will be opened at the judgment of the wicked dead. So it appears that God has some good methods of recording. This should challenge all of us to walk circumspectly before our God.

Chapter 12
Summary of My Ministry

*A*t the time when I was struggling with the call to preach—feeling that I was called, yet not willing to surrender—my English teacher, Miss Conrad, asked me to enter the high school oratorical contest. I was too timid to enter the contest, but I was never good at saying no, so I let her talk me into it. Of all things, she gave me a sermon by D. L. Moody to memorize and recite in the contest. Dutifully I memorized the sermon, and she coached me on how to stand and how to speak.

The night of the contest, most of the students and many of the townspeople were there. I was a freshman competing against seniors, but I did my best. Later they told me the judges wanted to award me first place, but they were reluctant to choose a freshman over a senior. That did a lot for my ego.

My pastor heard me that night. Soon after that I answered the call to preach, and the next Wednesday night he invited me to speak at his prayer meeting. A week later, I went with him to a revival he was holding in the Baptist Church at Mitchellsburg. The second night he asked me to preach. So I started preaching almost from the day I answered the call.

That summer I engaged in revival work. I preached and led singing in meetings through most of the summer, and I had good crowds and good results. I had no meetings after the first of September. Through the fall and winter, I studied my Bible, read books by Moody and others and prayed for the Lord to open doors for me.

Without my knowing it, the Lord was already working on my behalf. The night my pastor asked me to preach at Mitchellsburg, the Lord gave us a good service, and the people did not forget me. Several months later, after their pastor had resigned, they talked among themselves about me and wondered how to get in touch with me.

About that time one of the ladies from the church visited a home about twenty miles from Mitchellsburg. I frequently visited in the home next door. In conversation, the visitor mentioned that their church was looking for a pastor, and they told her about the young preacher who sometimes visited next door.

"Tell him to contact us," the visitor said, though she had no idea I was the young preacher they wanted to locate.

Before long I was told of the conversation, and I decided to help the people of the church find me. I drove to Mitchellsburg and asked how to get in touch with one of the church leaders.

I was told that Howard Preston was one of the deacons, and that he was working on the road on the other side of the knob.

I drove my car up the knob, but when I started down the other side, the road was muddy and torn up. So I parked and started walking. Halfway down the knob, I saw a man walking toward me, laughing.

"Where in the world did you come from?" he called when I was in hearing distance.

"I heard you people are looking for a pastor," I called back.

"We are."

We met and shook hands.

"When can you preach for us?" he asked.

"Next Sunday."

"I'll announce that you're coming, and we'll be expecting you."

I preached for them the next Sunday, and they called me to be their pastor. A week later, I preached at Salem Baptist Church. It was located about two miles from where I had met Howard Preston. They also called me to be their pastor. I accepted both churches as half-time charges, and I was in the ministry full-time. I have been in the ministry full-time ever since.

I came to know and love the people of both churches, and many fond memories of those days remain with me.

At that time Mitchellsburg, a crossroads village, boasted a railroad station, a post office, two stores, three churches and perhaps twenty-five or thirty houses.

As I recall the attendance at Mitchellsburg was not more than 35 when I became pastor, but I could not have been more excited if it had been a thousand.

The attendance did not long remain at 35, and, by the time I held my own revival that summer, both the building and the yard were filled with people. Many people were converted while I was at Mitchellsburg, and the church grew greatly. The people were patient with a young, inexperienced pastor, but some of them were not above putting me in my place when they thought I had stepped out of bounds.

Salem Baptist Church was in the country on Scrub Grass Creek. On cold winter Sundays, when my car would not start, I walked the three miles from Mitchellsburg, where I had moved, and I crossed the creek four or five times on the way, by placing stepping stones in the creek and crossing carefully on them.

On such Sundays the attendance was small, and we huddled around the old potbellied heating stove, and sang and prayed, and studied God's Word. After Sunday school, I preached to them. In the good weather of spring, summer, and fall, the attendance was good for a country church. Often the church was filled, and God gave us some blessed services.

The people at Salem loved me, fed me on Sundays, challenged me, and sometimes tried me. I remember a lady (name unknown) shaking hands with me at the door one Sunday morning and saying, "That was a nice little talk. If you keep on trying, someday you'll make a preacher." That really punctured my balloon. Here I was, a young D. L. Moody, and she had just called my great sermon, "a little talk."

I had a lot to learn when I started pastoring at Mitchellsburg and Salem, but the people put up with my blunders, encouraged me, and prayed for me. The Lord knocked some of the rough edges off a young, country preacher while I was there, and I became a better preacher because He did.

I remember a talk I had with the Lord one day as I climbed the knob on foot, on my way from Salem to Mitchellsburg. I asked the Lord to give me the power He had given D. L. Moody. It seemed that the Lord said to me, "Son, when you get Moody's crowd, I'll give you Moody's power. For the present, I'll give you all the power you need to pastor Mitchellsburg and Salem Baptist Churches."

After I left the pastorates at Mitchellsburg and Salem, I pastored in Garrard County, then in Madison County. After that I went to the First Baptist Church in Inez, in the mountains of East Kentucky. While I was in East Kentucky, I organized the Warfield Baptist Church from a meeting I held there in an abandoned church building. More than 80 people were baptized and became charter members of the church.

When I moved in the parsonage at Inez, I reserved one small room for an office. I had a used portable typewriter I had bought for $10.00, but I did not have a desk. I had to make do with an old kitchen table. I longed for a desk, but I did not have money to buy one, nor did I have money to buy the lumber to build one.

Times were hard during the early years of my ministry, and my income was small. When I moved to the First Baptist Church at Inez, it did not increase greatly. That church, despite its name, was a mission church. The Kentucky Baptist State Mission Board supplemented the small salary they paid. Even with the mission board's help, the salary was far from adequate.

After I had been at Inez about a year, one of my members started building a house next door to the parsonage. Each day the carpenters threw out scraps of lumber, and I started wondering if there would be any scraps large enough for me to use to build a desk. To my despair they threw out nothing that was large enough.

One day, about the time they were finishing the house, some workmen delivered a new refrigerator in a wooden shipping crate. My new neighbor removed the crate and threw it out with the scrap lumber. The minute I saw that crate, I started wondering if I could make a desk of it. I turned it on its side and saw that it was made of very thin plywood, reinforced at the corners by one inch strips of rough lumber.

The crate had been strong enough to contain the refrigerator while it was shipped across the country. Surely it would be strong enough to make a desk, I reasoned. I would only have to cut it to the needed size, cut out a place in the front for my knees, cut openings for the drawers, and make a strong top for it.

More excited than I wanted my neighbor to realize, I asked him if I could have the crate and some of the scrap lumber to use to make a desk.

Looking devious, he said I could take what I needed. So I carried the crate home and started working on it.

I had no power tools, and the few hand tools I had were old and dull, so it was hard work and slow. I cut the crate to the size of a desk, cut an opening for my knees and openings for the drawers—two on each side and one above the knee opening. I ripped lumber for the drawer slides. I built the drawers from some larger scraps. Then I went to the grocery store and asked for some empty wooden apple crates. From these I made drawer fronts.

I found some short pieces of flooring and used them to make the top of the desk. I used pieces of molding to reinforce the corners and to cover the rough edges of the top. When the desk was finished, my only expense had been for a few finish nails. Then I had to come up with enough money to buy sandpaper, putty, oil stain, varnish, and some inexpensive plastic drawer pulls.

It must have taken me a day or two to hand sand all the rough places off the desk. Then I stained it with cherry oil stain. The stain was much redder than cherry. It really was bright after I varnished it, but I still thought it was a beautiful desk.

After the varnish dried, I put the drawer pulls on, and my desk was finished. I moved it to the room I was using for an office, then put paper, envelopes, pencils, and paper clips in the drawers. I placed the portable typewriter on top of the desk, brought a chair from the kitchen, and I was in business.

No preacher could ever have been more pleased with a desk than I was with mine. I used that desk when I was preparing sermons, answering mail, and keeping records. I even wrote the first draft of my first novel and the beginning of several others on that desk.

When I moved to my next church, I moved that desk with me. Through the years, I have continued to move it everywhere I have gone.

While I was pastor in Ashland, Kentucky, a few years later, I bought a chair to match the desk, and I thought I really was getting up in the world. I have a picture of me, made after I moved from Ashland to Central Kentucky, sitting at the desk, looking very pastoral.

I am not sure when I finally got prosperous enough to buy a regular desk, but the day did come. A few years ago, I bought the large desk I am now using. It is great for the work I do, but it will never invoke the memories that my first desk does.

After leaving Inez, I pastored in Johnson and

Pike counties before going to Central Baptist Church in Ashland, Kentucky. From Central Baptist, I moved to a South Elkhorn Baptist Church in Fayette County.

After resigning at South Elkhorn, I organized the Rosemont Baptist Church in Lexington at the close of a two week revival. The church located on the south side of the city.

I left Rosemont to go into evangelism for a time. Later I organized the Fellowship Baptist Church on the north end of Lexington. For a time Fellowship Baptist worshiped in a rented building. After that building burned, we bought property and built an auditorium that would seat around 1800 people.

The day we dedicated Fellowship Baptist Church, an estimated four thousand tried to attend. Cars filled the parking lot and every available space on nearby streets. They blocked all roads leading to the church.

Fellowship Baptist Church grew like a weed. Soon people were coming from every adjoining county every Sunday. They overworked the men in charge of parking and kept several ushers busy seating them. People were constantly saved and united with the church. In one period of 18 months, we did not miss a single service (including prayer meetings) seeing people saved. Often on Sunday mornings 10 to 25 people came forward to receive the Lord as Savior.

At that time my daily radio broadcast blanketed Central Kentucky. That was before TV

came to the region, and there were not many radio stations to divide the audience. Almost everybody listened to our program. I'm sure it was
a contributing factor to the rapid growth of the
church.

The following is an example of the power of
radio in those days. In January, I scheduled a
Sunday afternoon service in the courthouse at
Danville, Kentucky. I announced the service on
my daily radio program and on the Sunday programs. I may have placed a small ad in the
Danville paper.

On the Saturday night before the planned service, a blizzard struck Central Kentucky. It
brought freezing rain and sleet. By Sunday morning all roads were ice-coated and almost impassible. I doubted that anyone would venture out
for the service in Danville in such weather and
on such hazardous roads, but I felt obligated to
go.

After a hurried lunch we started driving to
Danville on the ice-coated roads. We started early,
but the roads were so bad it was past time for the
service to start when we reached the courthouse.
To my amazement, I saw people lined up for a
city block trying to get into the building. I thought
perhaps the door was locked, but when I reached
the door, I found that it was blocked with people.
And the stairway leading to the courtroom on the
second floor was packed with people. They were
standing four abreast on each stair tread. The
courtroom was also packed with people.

I had to go to the rear of the building and go up a back stairway to reach the crowded courtroom. When I entered, a deacon from the First Baptist Church stood up and got my attention.

"There is no way this crowd can get in here, and it's too cold for people to stand outside," he said. "The First Baptist Church is directly behind the courthouse. I'll go open the door so you can have the service there. Tell the people on the stairway to turn around and go down so the people in here can get out. They can all march around the block to the church."

I made the announcement, and the people at the head of the stairs relayed the word to the ones below them. They passed the word along to the people outside the door, and they passed the word to those who were lined up along the block. Those at the end of the line started walking toward the church, and the others followed. I doubt that I lost anyone in the move.

Soon the large auditorium and balcony of the First Baptist Church were filled. There were many standing after all the seats were taken.

The service started late, but no one seemed to mind. I had great liberty preaching, and the presence of the Lord was very real in the service. More than 25 adults came forward to receive Christ as Savior. My radio ministry brought that great crowd together in spite of the ice storm, and God truly blessed.

In my years of ministry, I had the joy of organizing nine churches and of seeing other churches grow out of my ministry. I pastored some of the churches I organized, two in Cincinnati, one in Louisville, four in Lexington, and one in Campbellsville.

In the 1950s and 1960s, I did mission work in Mexico, Central America, Jamaica, Barbados and the Bahamas. I saw many souls saved on these mission fields.

This summary is far from complete, but it gives a glimpse of some aspects of the busy schedule the Lord has enabled me to keep through the years.

Chapter 13
Travel in My Early Days

*I*n my lifetime, I have traveled in every way a person can travel except by submarine and rocket ship. Early in life I was introduced to travel on horseback and muleback and by buggy, buckboard, and wagon. Later I traveled by automobile, truck, bus, and train. I also traveled by sailboats, fuel-powered boats, and airplanes. I have even ridden camelback on more than one occasion. That is the form of riding I like the least. A camel has the gait of a broken rocking chair, the breath of a waterfront bum, and the disposition of a mama grizzly bear.

In my early years, most people depended on a horse and buggy to get around. Buggies were big business in those days. Before Papa and Mama were married, he helped build buggies in Danville, Kentucky in a factory owned and operated by his brother, Roy. One of those buggies is on display at the Kentucky Horse Park, near Lexington. It is possible that Papa worked on that buggy when he was a young man.

My grandparents owned a buggy before our

family did. I remember riding with my grandmother in their buggy, pulled by a big sorrel horse named Ol' Rolly. Happily I sat by her, talking, enjoying the ride, and watching the miles go by.

When the weather was cold, we wrapped ourselves in a buggy rug, and we put a hot brick in the floor of the buggy to keep our feet warm. In warm weather, we sometimes encountered an unexpected rain and had to get the storm curtain from under the seat and hurriedly put it up across the front of the buggy top. The curtain kept us almost dry, as we peered out through the isinglass window to see the road ahead.

The best trips were in warm, sunny weather. My grandmother used to hurry Ol' Rolly with the buggy whip, which was mounted in a holder on the dashboard. It was my delight to use the whip to coax Ol' Rolly to go faster when he loitered.

Before Mama and Papa got a buggy, we rode on our mare, Liz, and our mule, Jack. We only had one horse. Mama rode sidesaddle on the mare, and Papa rode astride the mule. I usually rode behind Papa, holding onto him. Ol' Jack was gentle, but his gait was rough. I felt as if I were going to be homogenized (though I didn't know the word) before we reached the end of a journey. Liz was a saddle mare. It was a pleasure to ride her, though I seldom got the chance.

Finally the day came when Papa went to Danville and brought home a new Arnold Buggy he had bought from my uncle. It was black and shiny, and I thought it was beautiful. I climbed up into the seat, and Papa took me for a drive out to the pike and back.

We enjoyed driving Liz and the buggy to Lancaster to shop and to my grandparents' home to visit. We even went to Danville in the buggy on some occasions.

After we had had the buggy several years, Papa took the top off. I never knew why. Maybe it was just worn out. For the benefit of our young readers, when a buggy no longer had a top, it was called a buckboard—why I do not know. A buckboard looked like a dune buggy with bicycle wheels that was drawn by a horse.

We used that buckboard for several years. Mama and Papa used to ride in the seat, and I knelt in the floor with my hands on the dashboard and pretended I was driving a car. I drove many a mile that way.

Among my happiest memories were the times when we drove Liz and the buckboard to church in Lancaster. We started going to church there after I was converted. Mama and I enjoyed attending church, but Papa, not a Christian at that time, soon found an excuse to stop going.

Three miles of the trip to church was on the Richmond Road. It was a good, graveled road, but the ever increasing number of automobiles made the authorities decide to blacktop it. Country people called the blacktopped road, "the slick road." Right away Papa decided that a horse could fall and break a leg on "the slick road," so we stopped going to church. I have always thought it strange that we traveled the same slick road on Saturdays when we went to town to buy groceries, and nothing was said about the danger of the mare falling.

When I was eleven, a salesman came to our farm from Lancaster to try to sell Papa a Model-T Ford roadster. That was a car with one seat and a cloth top. They had to work to sell cars in those days. The car the salesman drove to our house was clean and shiny. In those days a customer could buy a car of any color he liked, just so long as it was black. So this car was black.

The salesman took Mama and Papa and me a ride in the car. He gave Papa his best sales pitch, but that did not persuade him to buy the car. At last the salesman left, but he came back the next day, and again the next day. Finally he wore Papa down. Mama may have helped change his mind. At any rate, Papa decided it would be nice to own a car. He must have done some figuring during those three days—trying to decide where he would get money to pay for the car.

The price of the car was four hundred and eight dollars, lot of money in those days. Papa sold a cow and half of mama's chickens and drew most of his money from the bank, and he came up with enough to pay cash for the car.

Papa bought the car with all the options they offered. They called them extras in those days, and they only offered two. One was called a self-starter. That meant that instead of cranking the car and taking a chance on the balky thing kicking backwards and breaking your arm, you could stamp on a stiff starter button in the floor, back by the seat, until you got a bruise on your heel. Either way, at the threat of life and limb, you could start the car.

The other extra was called demountable rims. That was supposed to make it easier to fix a flat tire. We had lots of flat tires in those days. Before demountable rims came out, tires were mounted on a rim that was part of the wheel. So you had to fix a flat tire in the hot sun, if it was summertime, and you had to take a chance on someone running over you while you were fixing it. The demountable rim fixed all that—that is, most of it.

The demountable rim was fastened to the wheel by four lug nuts. So it was relatively easy to remove. All you had to do was chock the other wheels, so the car wouldn't roll off the jack after the wheel with the flat was jacked up. A special wrench to remove the lug nuts was furnished with the car.

After removing the lug nuts, you could lift the rim and tire off and carry them to the shade of a tree where you could work with tire irons (also furnished with the car) and strain and struggle for an hour to get the tire off the rim. By that time you were wet with perspiration and as dirty as if you had rolled in a horse-wallow. And you wished you were anywhere but where you were. There is no point in going into the grueling details of how we used to fix flat tires. Few of my readers will ever want to try it anyway. So, I'll simply say, for better or for worse, Papa bought a car with demountable rims.

We went back to church after we got the car. The slick road didn't bother the car at all. It rather seemed to like it. To say the least, the car liberated us. We went to church, and we went places we had never been before. We even went to camp meeting in the next county. I had never before been out of the county I was born in. We even went to visit my mother's sister and her family on Poosey Ridge in Madison County. Later, after they moved to Lexington, we visited them there.

While we were in Lexington, we went walking on Main Street, and Mama pointed out the First National Bank building to me and told me that it was a skyscraper. I looked up at it for a long minute. Then I said: "Gee, Mama, I'd like to see it work."

I learned to drive the new Ford in mud holes. Papa wouldn't let me touch the wheel out on the road, but when he got the car stuck in the mud between the house and barn, he let me under the wheel so I could put the car in gear and give it gas while he pushed. With Papa pushing, the car usually came out of the mud, and I always drove it to the beginning of the graveled drive in front of the house. I thought I could drive as well as anyone by the time I was twelve.

You might say I had a love affair with cars,

especially with Fords. I took to them like a duck to water. Within months I was working on our car and on my grandmother's touring car. She bought hers a year before we bought ours. I learned to clean spark plugs and carburetors, to change distributors, to put on fan belts, to adjust the band linings in the transmission, and to adjust the spark gap in the four coils that were in a box inside the fire wall. That was about all that ever had to be done to a Model-T, short of an overhaul. Papa and I eventually learned to do that also.

To this day I remember the slow rhythm of an idling Model-T motor when both the spark and gas levers were pushed all the way up. And I remember how each coil would give a slight buzzing sound as it furnished spark to the plug it was wired to.

When I was about fifteen, I started wanting a car of my own, but of course there was no money to buy me a car, even if Papa had been of a mind to do so. In those days, when a car was well-worn, boys and young men used to buy them and take the old battered, rusty body off. They bolted a wood platform on the chassis and bolted a seat to it under the steering wheel. They called this kind of vehicle a skeeter. A skeeter was much lighter than a car, so it would outrun any car on the road.

Often people who had skeeters put a cutout on them. In case you don't already know, a cutout was a gadget they bolted on the exhaust pipe, after a hole had been cut in it. A control on the floor opened and closed the cutout. When a driver opened the cutout with a skeeter running wide open, it roared like a bulldozer. It wasn't any trouble to get other traffic out of the way, especially if a Claxton horn had been put on the skeeter. The loud AH-OO-GUH sound of a Claxton horn was sufficient to drive other traffic to the ditch. Cutouts and Claxton horns were sometimes installed on regular cars also.

Somehow I saved enough money to buy a skeeter when I was about sixteen, The going price back then was around $10.00 for a skeeter in running condition. I drove the skeeter for a few days, but I really was not satisfied with it. I wanted a regular car. About that time someone took a body off another Ford and left it on the roadside. I asked around and found the owner. He no longer wanted the body, so he gave it to me.

I got some other boys to help, and we stripped off the floor that had been added to the skeeter. Then we managed to get the car body in place on the chassis and bolted it down. There was only one small problem. The body was off a car that was a later model than my skeeter, so the running board brackets on the chassis were not long enough to reach the running boards on the body.

It never occurred to me to have longer brackets welded on the chassis, but I came up with my own solution. I found a 1 x 8 board long enough to reach from the outer edge of one running board to the outer edge of the other, underneath the car.

So I jacked each running board up to level and propped it in place. Then I measured from edge to edge and cut the board the proper length. I drilled holes in the running boards and in the board. Then I bolted the board in place and removed the props. The running boards stayed level, almost, but when I stepped on the running board on the driver's side, it went down several inches, and the one on the other side went up an equal distance. It was like an upside down seesaw. I got in the car, and, when my weight came off the running board, it returned to its normal place. I decided to take the car for a trial run. It performed perfectly, except for the running boards. They went up and down like the wings of a big bird, and each time they hit bottom, they made a loud screeching sound. I had no need for a cutout or a Claxton horn on that car. Everybody could hear me coming without them.

I do not remember what I did with my first car, but I well remember my second one. It was a later model Ford Touring Car that I bought for fifteen dollars. It was in fair mechanical condition, but some previous owner had painted a large skull and crossbones across the back of it with white paint. They had used a brush about two inches wide, so a driver following me could see that skull and crossbones almost before he saw the car. I never was comfortable driving that car, especially if some other young people went riding with me.

The Skull and Crossbones Car pulled a trick

on me that I have never forgotten. There was a mechanical curiosity about a T-model that I need to explain. Underneath the car there was a radius rod that ran between the front wheels. If by some mishap the radius rod got bent, it could be straightened, but it wouldn't stay straight, and a car with a bent radius rod behaved very strangely. It drove all right as long as the driver did not have to go around a sharp curve, but, when the steering wheel was turned beyond a certain point, the wheels would suddenly cut in the opposite direction, and the car would go out of control.

The Crossbones Car had a bent radius rod. I soon discovered it. So I drove it very carefully. One day some young people went riding with me on a country road. At a sharp curve, I must have forgotten about the bent radius rod and cut the car too short. Suddenly it went out of control and ran up a steep bank. I got it stopped at the top of the bank. The motor died, and the car ran back down the bank backwards. In the process it threw a tire off a front wheel, and the inner tube suddenly swelled up like a huge balloon. We sat and laughed as only young people can laugh. Then, of course, I had to let the air out of the tube and put the tire back on the wheel and pump it up with a hand pump. That was probably the last time I took anyone riding in that car.

Chapter 14
Travel in the Ministry

*E*arly in my ministry I learned that much travel is required in the Lord's work, and with the passing of the years, I have found that the need to travel has increased. When I started in the ministry, expenses were high and income was low, so I sometimes walked to my meetings or caught rides with others. Other times, I traveled in dilapidated old cars that often broke down on the road.

I often worked on my car during the week to get it ready to drive to church on Sunday. On one occasion, after I had worked on my car during the week, the front wheel fell off on Sunday as I turned a corner in a town near my church. Fortunately I was not driving fast at the time. Often the old cars I drove had poor tires. I remember a night when I had four flat tires returning from a meeting.

Years later, it became necessary for me to buy an interest in an airplane and learn to fly. The need to fly arose after I held a revival in a store-front mission in Cincinnati, Ohio, during World

War II. The meeting was very successful, and the people decided to organize a church. They asked me to help with the organization on a Sunday afternoon.

I was pastoring near Lexington. That was before the days of interstate highways, and I knew it would take four hours to drive to the mission in Cincinnati and another four hours to return. So it would not be possible for me to drive to Cincinnati after my morning service, help organize the church, and return to Lexington in time for my service in the evening. Besides, with gas rationing because of the war, I did not have gas for the trip. So I decided to charter a plane and fly to Cincinnati. Before that flight was over, I was hooked. I wanted to learn to fly.

The new church asked me to serve as co-pastor for a time, and that made me decide to buy a plane and learn to fly. The only thing that bothered me was what I imagined would be the impossible cost of buying a plane.

One day that week, I mentioned my thoughts about buying a plane to Mr. Harold Leggett, a Lexington engraver who frequently made halftones for me to use to print pictures in my paper. He told me that he had been thinking of learning to fly. He had even found a used plane that was for sale for 750 dollars. If I was interested, we could buy the plane in partnership. I could use it on Sundays, and he would use it during the week.

Neither of us knew anything about airplanes. If we had we would never have bought the one

he had found. But, since we were blissfully ig-
norant, we borrowed the money and bought the
plane. The plane would fly all right, and it was
relative safe, I think. We never had a serious accident with it, but it did leave some things to be
desired. The plane was a tandem Piper Cub,
Model J3. Those old Cubs, usually used as train-
ers, were real workhorses, but the one we bought
was not equipped as most of them were. Every
other Cub I have ever seen, except the one we
bought had a 65 horsepower engine. Ours had
only a 50 horsepower engine. And it was the only
single ignition airplane I ever saw. Piston powered engines, used in airplanes, all have dual ignition—two magnetos, two sets of ignition wires,
and two sets of spark plugs. The idea is that if
one ignition fails, the other one will keep the
plane flying. Our plane, we learned when it was
too late, had only one ignition. If it failed, we
were going down. But we had bought the plane,
so we flew it, and we never had a problem with
the ignition.

The low horsepower meant that our plane had
to have a longer runway to get off the ground
than other Cubs, but we managed. A previous
owner had installed a high speed prop on the
plane, so we really had an edge in speed over the
more powerful Cubs. Our plane had no radio, no
running lights, no cabin lights, and no naviga-
tional instruments, except a rather unreliable
compass. And it had no heater, so it was icy cold
in winter.

The days following the purchase of our plane were among the most exciting of my life. I soon learned to fly and got my student permit. I got approved for cross-country flying and started commuting between my churches every Sunday. I soon started flying to revival meetings in Kentucky and surrounding states.

My partner also learned to fly, and we had many happy experiences flying together. Though I have only seen him once since he moved to Texas many years ago, I have many fond memories of our association.

Each Sunday morning I phoned the airport and asked them to service the plane. After the morning service in my church, I drove to the airport and asked a line boy to help me get started. I transferred the lunch I had packed and my Bible to the plane. I went through the check list, inspecting the plane as all good pilots do. The line boy helped me untie the plane, and I got in and fastened the seat belt.

The line boy pulled the propeller to turn the engine over a time or two. Then he called, "Contact." I turned on the ignition, and called, "Contact," in return. He gave a quick pull on the propeller, and the engine started. I finished my checklist, ran up the engine, taxied out to the runway, and took off. I cleared the field and turned the plane north by the compass.

I ate my lunch on the way to Cincinnati. In less than an hour I crossed the Ohio River and landed at Lunkin Airport. A member of the church was there to meet me and drive me across the city to the church. After the service, I returned to the airport, refueled the plane, and took off for the flight home.

The flights each Sunday were uneventful during the summer, but with the coming of fall, the days grew shorter, and I started running short of daylight on my return trip. I realized that I would soon be getting back after dark.

The people at the airport told me that I would have to have running lights if I was going to fly after dark. It was not legal to fly after dark without them. Besides it was dangerous. That was the first time I realized that other planes had lights. My partner and I had running lights put on the Cub. At least that would keep another plane from colliding with me in the dark.

The days grew shorter, and when I was flying home from Cincinnati, I could see the shadows gathering in the valleys by the time I had flown a third of the way. I could see lights going on in houses and on storefronts, and I could see cars on the road with their headlights on. I would begin to worry.

The gas tank on the cub only held 12 gallons of gasoline, enough for about three hours of flying. When the gasoline was gone, the engine would stop, and I would go down, wherever I chanced to be. My only hope was to fly straight to the airport at Lexington.

I could not help worrying about getting off course. Suppose the wind had changed directions, and I had drifted off course? Suppose that little compass, bouncing around, was not accurate? I had no radio guidance system, never heard of one at that time. Suppose I should miss the airport and fly past it? I would crackup and kill myself. I would start praying, and I would begin to scan the darkening sky in the direction of the airport. I had to see the beacon light at the airport. The tension was building in the cockpit.

Then I saw a pinpoint of light in the direction of the airport. I waited, tensed, one hand on the throttle, the other on the control stick, my eyes on the spot where I had seen the light. Thirty seconds later, another flash of light.

I watched . . . a green flash, an amber, a green, an amber. I relaxed and pointed the nose of the plane at the flashing light. The continuing drone of the engine reassured me, and the flashing light told me that I was on course.

I was soon circling the control tower at Blue Grass Field. Because I had no radio, they had told me to box the tower—to fly rectangles around the tower. The man on duty in the tower looked up and said, "Here comes that crazy preacher flying his Bible," and he turned on the lights along the runway.

I circled the field, lined up with the runway, and started my glide toward the lights. The throttle was cut now. The engine was turning at no more than 1500 RPM. It was relatively quiet in the cockpit. The lights were coming up to meet me. Then the wheels bumped on the runway, and

I thanked God for the flashing lights that had guided me home.

Flying made me a kind of a celebrity. I was written up by the Associated Press because I commuted between my churches in my own plane. Perhaps I was one of the first pastors to do that. The publicity did not mean a lot to me, but I am glad I was able to reach people for the Lord by traveling that way.

Since that time, I have flown in many planes, even the big jets, but I have never had more fun or accomplished more good than I did while flying the J3 Cub. It enabled me to carry the gospel to places and to people I would not otherwise have reached.

Much as I loved flying in my own plane, I often found it necessary to travel in other ways. While I pastored in Cincinnati, I sometimes traveled to the church on the train. I have also traveled by rail to revivals and to Bible conferences, and I have traveled by train when doing mission work in foreign lands. I have enjoyed that mode of travel since the time my grandfather took me from Hyattsville to Lancaster, a three mile ride on the train, when I was a small boy.

One of the most interesting journeys I ever made was by sailboat. Some of the natives of the Bahama Islands took me a day's journey, from Grand Bahama to Water Key, in a small sailboat. There were three or more in our crew, and Rev. Roy Harrison, now deceased, traveled with me. The trip going was pleasant, but when we returned the next day, it was cold and the sea was boisterous. Brother Harrison and I spent most of the day down in the hole, hiding from the wind. It made me think of Jonah in the hole of the ship that carried him on the journey that ended with him in a whale's belly. God must have watched over us, for we made trip safely, and I had the joy of preaching to the entire population of the island, except for one blind man. I will write more of this trip in another chapter.

In recent years I have pulled a trailer to most of my meetings that have been within driving distance. It is a bit more of a hassle getting to the meetings that way, but the trailer is a great asset. It is my home away from home, and it serves as an office as well. Much of my writing is done in the trailer.

In all the miles I have traveled, by every means available, God has watched over me, and I have enjoyed great success, preaching to people in many parts of America and in foreign lands.

Chapter 15

My Second Airplane Almost Killed Me

*A*fter flying the J3 Cub for a couple of years, I decided I needed a better plane. I wanted a plane that was faster, seated more than two people, had better instruments, a radio, a heater, and more comfort. All that seemed out of my reach, but I finally found a used Stinson 105 that I could afford. The Stinson seated two people side by side and a third person on a jump seat in the back that was crowded into an enlarged luggage compartment. It had the other things I wanted, but it had one problem; it was underpowered. I bought it anyway.

Being underpowered meant that the .plane loved the ground. It used up most of a long runway before I could coax it into the air and drag it over the boundary fence. It was somewhat like a bumblebee. Mathematically speaking, a bumblebee is not supposed to be able to fly. Its body is too heavy for its wing span. The bumblebee doesn't know that, so it flies anyway. So my new plane managed to fly, just barely.

I had some good times in that plane, and I

had some close calls as well. Flying the old J3 Cub became second nature to me. I could fly it like a bird, and I did things with it that I could never do with another plane, certainly not with the Stinson. I came near killing myself in the Stinson a few times before I learned that. *". . . But God . . ."*

The Stinson was a beautiful plane, and I had a picture of a flying Bible painted on the side of the fuselage, along with the words, *The Flying Evangelist.*

In the early spring I flew the Stinson to Detroit, Michigan for a revival. I landed at the nearest airport to the church where I was to hold the meeting. The field had a graveled runway, and, since the spring thaw had not come, the ground under the gravel was frozen solid. I had no trouble landing and taxiing to a tie-down, where I could secure the plane.

Two weeks later, when I attempted to take off for the flight home, the ground had started thawing beneath the graveled surface of the runway. In Kentucky, a thaw starts at the top. In Michigan, the ground thaws below the surface first. Not knowing that, I almost cracked up the plane when I tried to take off.

A young man decided to fly to Lexington with me. For some reason, our departure was delayed until afternoon. When we reached the airport, we loaded our bags in the plane. I had the plane serviced, did the usual inspection, had the line boy crank the plane, and taxied out for takeoff.

At the end of the runway, I turned into the wind and opened the throttle to start my takeoff run. Just as the plane started forward, the thawing ground gave way, and the wheels broke through the gravel into the mud. The plane stopped moving. The propeller blast lifted the tail off the ground, and the plane started nosing over. My hand was on the throttle, and instantly I cut the power. If I had not, the plane would have nosed over and landed on its back.

In spite of my quick action, the tip of the propeller struck the gravel before the tail wheel dropped back on the runway. The propeller was not seriously damaged, but the manager of the field insisted that I taxi to the shop and let his mechanic check it before I tried to take off again. He got enough help to push the plane out of the mud and to the shop.

There was really nothing wrong with the propeller, but the mechanic sanded a small rough place from it. He delayed me for a considerable time, and he did not forget to charge for what he had done.

Finally he pronounced the plane safe to fly, and I was directed to a more solid takeoff area. This time I took off without difficulty, but I realized that the delay might keep me from reaching Lexington before dark.

Once I was in the air, I encountered a strong head wind. That slowed our progress, and I soon realized that I could run out of fuel and daylight, before we reached Lunkin airport in Cincinnati, where I planned to land and refuel. Even if my fuel lasted long enough for me to get there, I did not have landing lights, and my radio was almost inoperable.

My instinct told me to fly fast and get as far as I could before dark, but my training told me to slow the airplane to conserve fuel. I pulled back on the throttle enough to slow the engine RPM, but not enough to lose flying speed. I did not tell my passenger that I was worried, but I kept looking for an airport were I could land and refuel, even though my chart indicated that there was none along my route. I knew that if I did not find an airport, I might have to make a forced landing in a rough, muddy field, and it would soon be too dark to make a forced landing.

Frantically I looked for a town large enough to have a flying field. Maybe there would be an airport that was not on the chart, or maybe I was off course and would just happen to fly over an airport.

I watched the dropping needle on my gas gauge, and I watched the fading daylight that came into the cockpit from the overcast sky. My nerves were growing more taunt by the minute. I knew it was time to pray, and I knew that I must soon make a decision. I must either attempt to land on an unlikely field, or I must trust my dwindling gas supply to get me to a town with a landing field, maybe Cincinnati.

I did not want to frighten my passenger, so I prayed silently, "Dear Lord, please tell me what to do." I continued to pray as the plane sliced through the gathering gloom. The ground below me was now rough and hilly. There was no likely field in sight where I could safely land the plane, so I kept flying.

Night came almost suddenly. It appeared to drop out of the overcast sky and to envelope us. Now the die was cast. I had to keep flying and hoping that my dwindling gas supply would last until I could find a lighted airport.

I switched on the cockpit light and the running lights, knowing that we were in real trouble. I flew on, watching the gas gauge, the compass and the horizon—praying, knowing that only the Lord could guide us to a safe landing.

Before long the fuel gauge was bumping empty, and I listened for any miss in the engine that would signal the last of the fuel. The steady roar of the engine was small comfort, for I knew that soon the roar could become a sputter. Then the engine would stop.

At that moment I saw blinking lights ahead, several of them. They were randomly spaced over a wide area, and none of them appeared to be a beacon at a landing field. They did indicate, however, that I was approaching a city, and maybe, just maybe, one of them would guide me to a landing field.

I did not have enough fuel to fly to the lights one by one and check them. Perhaps I did not have enough to fly to even one of them. I looked at the gauge. It was still moving—barely. I had to fly to the right beacon—if there was a right beacon.

"Dear Lord, guide me," I prayed. Then I selected one of the lights and started toward it. It was not a beacon light for an airport, I knew, but I felt led to fly to it.

The gas gauge stopped moving, but the engine kept roaring on, boring through the night. Minutes passed, then I saw a concrete runway below me. If it had been a grass or blacktop runway, I would never have seen it. Unstained concrete reflects just enough light, even on an overcast night, to make it visible.

There were no lights around the field, so it must be closed for the night, I concluded. I could not see if there were obstructions—power lines, smokestacks, or tall buildings around the field—so I decided to descend to a few hundred feet above ground and line up with the runway. I would approach the runway in a glide, slightly above landing speed, and when I was sure I had passed the boundary of the field, I would cross the controls and slip the plane to lose altitude rapidly, a safe enough maneuver in daylight, but it would be tricky in the dark. If I made it safely to the proximity of the runway, I would pull the plane out of the slip and try for a landing on a runway I would probably not be able to see.

The engine droned on as I circled the field to line up with the runway. Suddenly a huge spotlight came on, near the ground at one end of the runway. It was shining down the runway and

straight into my eyes. Almost blinded, I kept going. If my gas would only last, I would fly around
behind that light and approach the runway from
that direction. That way I could see the runway.
I prayed that my fuel would last.

The engine droned on and the prop kept turning. When I got behind the light, I had to almost
feel my way toward the boundary of the field in
the darkness. I hoped I was high enough to avoid
hitting any unseen obstructions, and not too high
to land after I crossed the boundary. Tension was
so thick in the cockpit, you could have sliced it.
I knew that I would only have one pass at that
runway. I had to do this one right.

After I passed the light at the boundary, I could
see the runway below me, too far below me. I
cut the throttle and put the plane in a steep slip
toward the runway, knowing that I had to lose
altitude quickly, or I would overshoot the field. I
could hear the wind slicing past the plane. I was
flying by the seat of my pants.

The plane slid downward, near a stall. The
runway was coming up at me. I brought the controls back to normal, and the plane righted itself.
I dropped the nose slightly, then pulled back on
the wheel, feeling the plane slow and settle. A
short eternity. Then the wheels bumped the runway. Ah, blessed land. Terra firma!

I turned and taxied toward a building, now
visible in the glare of the floodlight. Two men
came out to meet me and my almost forgotten
passenger. They pumped our hands, feeling good

that they had made it possible for us to make a safe landing.

"We should have been gone long before we heard your plane," one of them said. "We had been closed a long time, but we just kept hanging around talking, something we have never done before."

I don't remember what I told them, but I know that the Lord had kept them there to turn the light on for us.

Not long after I bought the Stinson, the Gulf Oil Corporation offered free gas and oil to any private pilot who would fly to the air races in Miami. I signed up for the trip, and agreed to paste the Gulf Oil Company's logo on the cowling of my plane. I had never been to Florida, and, loving flying the way I did, I considered this the chance of a lifetime.

Brother Roy Edwards, my deacon and long-time friend from Salem Baptist Church, decided to go with me. We must have been delayed getting started, for it was mid-afternoon when we landed in Georgia to refuel. Because it was late, and because we were in a hurry, I did not check behind the serviceman to see that he had done his job properly.

"Fill both tanks with gas and check the oil," I told him. "And be sure that the oil cap is firmly seated," I called over my shoulder as Roy and I started inside.

When we returned, I asked the serviceman if he was sure the oil cap was firmly seated, and he assured me that it was. I knew that the plane would throw the oil out if the cap was not tight, but I did not check behind him.

Roy and I took off, climbed to cruising altitude, and again headed south. We had not been flying more than half an hour when I noticed that the RPM of the engine was dropping.

Automatically I pulled the carburetor heat on, in case the engine was icing up. At the same instant, I glanced at the instrument panel and saw that there was no oil pressure. Instantly I knew that the serviceman had not tightened the oil cap. Sick at heart, I turned off the ignition, hoping against hope that I had not already ruined the engine.

The propeller stopped turning, and it was very quiet in the cockpit. I could hear the wind as the plane cut through it. I started looking for a field large enough to land in.

"What's wrong?" Roy asked calmly, though I doubt that he was feeling calm.

"We had no oil pressure, so I had to stop the engine."

"This is going to be rough, isn't it?" he asked.

"Not really. We are flying over level country, and there are some big fields down there. I always land with the engine idling. This won't be much different from a normal landing," I answered, trying to reassure him.

Below me was a grass field large enough to land an airliner in, but it was full of cattle. My landing plane could stampede them, and they might cause me to crash. Even if they didn't, they could damage the plane before I could get oil and take off again. Next to that field was a large last-year's cornfield. The corn had been picked, but the stalks were still standing. I decided that the stalks would do less damage to the plane than the cows, so I circled the cornfield, turned into the wind and lined up with the corn rows. Slowly I glided down and landed. The plane bumped a time or two on the rough ground and rolled to a stop. I looked at Roy and he smiled a weak smile.

We got out and pushed the plane to the end of the field and tied it to the fence. Then we found a phone and called for help.

We had landed near Albany, Georgia. Some mechanics came out and checked the engine. It had to be rebuilt, so they removed it and took it to shop at the airport.

Roy and I decided to go on to Florida on a bus. We made a tour down one coast and up the other. Then Roy went home, and I returned to Albany to get my plane. Because I had been care-less, I was a wiser and a poorer man when I flew home from Albany.

The forced landing in Georgia was child's play compared to what happened to me on a win-ter day when I attempted to fly to Louisville for an evangelistic conference.

The morning I was to fly to the conference, I phoned the weather bureau and inquired about flying conditions. They told me there was noth-ing to be concerned about, though they were expecting some widely-scattered snow flurries. Reassured, I drove to Cool Meadow Airport, where the Stinson was based. I got the plane out of the hanger and had it serviced. This time, of course, and all future times, I personally saw that the oil cap and the gas caps were properly seated. Then I ran my preflight inspection and my checklist, started the plane, and taxied out for takeoff.

I used most of the grass runway, because of the underpowered engine, before I lifted the plane into the air. I cleared the trees beyond the boundary fence, then dropped the nose, as I had to with that plane, to let it gain flying speed. Just then a blinding snowstorm closed around me, and I could not see beyond the windshield.

Fear stabbed at me as I remembered the radio tower directly ahead of me. Instinctively, I pulled back on the control wheel to climb over it. An airplane in flight has its own center of gravity, so with the ground not visible, I had no way of knowing the attitude of the plane, whether it was flying level, climbing, turning or diving. I had blind flight instruments, but I was not trained to use them. I did not even think to look at them. My only thought was to get over that tower.

Speed is what makes a plane lift off the ground and fly. When the speed drops below flying speed, the plane stalls and starts toward the ground nose first. It may even get in a spin and spin to the ground like a corkscrew.

When I pulled back on the wheel, the Stinson stalled. Suddenly I heard the engine roaring louder than usual, and, in a panic, I realized that I was in a dive—straight toward the ground with only two or three hundred feet to go. I glanced at the airspeed indicator and saw that I was doing 140 MPH, and the airspeed was climbing. The tachometer was past the red danger mark and climbing. I knew I had only seconds before crashing into the ground—and sudden death.

"Lord save me," I cried.

At that instant it felt as if God's hands were controlling my hands. Then I felt the pullout, and I felt as if I were going through the seat. I feared that the wings would break off the plane, and that it would disentegrate in the air. " . . . *But God.*"

The plane stayed together, and now it had plenty of speed to climb. I looked at the blind flight instruments and used the little knowledge I had of them to keep the plane flying safely. When I had reached a safe altitude, I turned the plane, ever so gently. I did what pilots call a 180 and flew out of the snow squall. I flew back to the airport and landed. Then I got on my knees and thanked the Lord for saving my life. I still praise Him for saving my life and for letting me live all these years to preach the gospel.

Chapter 16

Preaching from the Sky

*T*here was a time when I made a most unique use of a small plane. In 1948 one of the radio stations carrying my daily broadcast was WFKY in Frankfort, Kentucky. Through the broadcast on that station I became acquainted with Clark Karsner and his family.

Clark was operating a flight school from a small airport on his farm at Monterey, not far from Frankfort, and was training pilots on the GI Bill. Perhaps because I owned and flew a plane, and because we were both interested in spreading the gospel, Clark and I became good friends.

Clark gave considerable support to my radio ministry, and one day he came to me with another idea for spreading the gospel. He suggested that we preach from an airplane over a powerful loud speaker. I was skeptical. I thought that the plane would pass over an area so quickly that people on the ground would not hear enough of the message for it to have any effect on them.

Clark had evidently been in touch with the

Lord about the matter, and he was convinced that it would work.

I had another objection. There was no loud speaker built that had enough power to carry the message from the plane to the ground. Besides, I did not know of an easy way to power such an amplifier if we had one.

Clark had already looked into that. He had found an electronics man who would build a loud speaker with the needed power, and he would build a power supply from army surplus parts to power it. Clark offered to pay for the system and have it installed on one of his planes. Then he would fly it every afternoon, when the weather was good enough for people to be outside, and he would beam the message down to them.

"How can I ride with you in such an overloaded plane and do the preaching?" I asked.

He had an answer for that also. That was before the days of tape recorders, but RCA had come out with a wire recorder. He was sure that we could record the messages on it, and he could play it back over the loud speaker.

I still was not convinced, but it was his money, and if he wanted to spend it that way, I was willing to go along.

In a short time the electronics man built the loud speaker. My, what a contraption it was. It looked like we would need a pickup truck to move it. Mounted on the main amplifier were several radio tubes. The output tubes were enormous. Also, there was a huge, war-surplus dynamotor to power it. The army must have used it to power field transmitters. The dynamotor alone weighed about 75 pounds. And there was a mammoth storage battery, the largest one I had ever seen. There were two big horns with brackets to bolt them on the wing-struts of the plane. The RCA wire recorder probably weighed another 75 pounds. When all that equipment was loaded in the small Aronica trainer, there was barely room for Clark to squeeze into his seat. The plane was so overloaded, we had to fly it under an experimental license.

I still wondered if we could reach people in this way, but I went to Clark's home to record the first message to be broadcast from The Gospel Plane. Mrs. Karsner played the piano and sang a verse of a song. Then I preached a two minute sermon.

The following week Clark flew The Gospel Plane to a different town each afternoon, slowed the plane to the slowest possible flying speed, turned on the loud speaker and the recorder, and circled as the message blasted down. The response was immediate and, to me, surprising. I heard of a man who stopped on the street of his hometown and listened to the singing and preaching coming down from the plane. "I wonder how in the world they got that piano up there in that plane," he remarked.

The next Sunday morning, when I gave the invitation in my church in Lexington, a handsome young farmer came down the aisle and took my hand.

"I have been converted," he began. "I want to join the church and be baptized, but I have to tell you how it happened. One day last week, I was working in my barn when I heard singing coming down from above. I ran out of the barn, still carrying the pitchfork I had been using, and looked up. I saw the plane and stood there by the barn door and listened to the message. After the plane was gone, I bowed my head and asked the Lord to save me."

Soon I heard of a man who stopped his truck on the streets of Lexington and stood beside it listening to the message from The Gospel Plane. He also trusted Jesus as his Savior. In a village near Lexington, several people fell on their knees and called on the Lord for salvation. A black man told me how he had heard singing from the air as he worked, laying the walls of the basement for a house. He thought the Lord was coming, and he dropped his tools, ran home, got on his knees, and asked the Lord to save him.

Numbers of people wrote me their impressions of The Gospel Plane. A few of their letters are included.

I was all but overwhelmed this morning as I sat reading my Bible, when suddenly out of the blue I recognized your voice ringing out, *"As it was in the days of Noah."* Oh how we need to hear that message.

With my Bible in my hand, I walked out into the yard and listened, wishing in my heart that I couod be up there with you, helping proclaim the gospel news.

Keep up the good work. I have predicted that you will prove to be a Moody, a Spurgeon, a Sunday, or a Whitfield. Gentleman, Kentucky.

I heard you the other day as your plane circled over Nicholasville. It brought tears to my eyes ... I have heard all kinds of advertising from planes, but never before have I heard the Word of God from a plane. Lady, Kentucky.

I was in Georgetown Tuesday afternoon and heard your airplane and the gospel message. I told my daughter that's what I call stepping out for Jesus. Lady, Kentucky.

I just have to write after hearing you in the air yesterday. It sounded so good, but it sure put many thoughts in my mind about the last days. Lady, Kentucky.

I think your preaching from the air is the greatest thing I ever heard of. People will hear who have never heard the gospel in any other way. Man and wife, Kentucky.

Reprint From Lockland Baptist Witness

The Lockland Baptist Witness was a paper published by the Lockland Baptist Church when Rev. Ben Hillard was pastor. Lockland Baptist Church is now Landmark Baptist Temple, where Dr. John Rawlings is pastor. Under the leadership of Dr. Rawlings, the church has long since bought some of the most beautiful property in any city and located on it: Ed. Note.

Louis Arnold owns his private airplane. He not only flies it to and from his engagements in churches, preaching revivals, etc., but now has rigged up his plane with an amplifier and is preaching the gospel over Lexington, Kentucky and other cities.

I have read about the Devil being *"the prince of the power of the air."* Louis Arnold has accepted the Devil's challenge to the sole right of the air, and is heralding glad tidings of redemptive joy from the ether regions. This is most interesting, since most religious programs have been denied the use of radio.

It will be a miracle if the Devil and his gang do not seek to prevent Brother Arnold from spreading the gospel as he soars through the air. It will indeed be interesting to know what they could do about it.

> More power to the man who rises
> above the earth's solid surface to preach
> the gospel. —Lockland Baptist Witness

Because of The Gospel Plane, I was invited by Baptista Films to come to their studios in Wheaton, Illinois to be filmed for a movie, *Voice From the Sky*. After I made my part of the movie, they sent a camera crew and a director to Lexington to finish filming. For many years this movie was available to churches throughout the United States.

I still meet people who trusted the Lord after hearing the message from the plane. Recently, when I visited a church in Lexington, a lady told me that she had been ironing when she heard the message from the sky and trusted the Lord.

Clark Karsner went home to be with the Lord a few years ago. Now his son, Don, is preaching the gospel and is a successful pastor.

What a joy it will be when I get home and rejoice with Clark and his good wife and his preacher son and the souls who were saved because of Clark's idea and his faithfulness in flying the plane with a message.

Chapter 17

Mission Work in the Islands

*A*fter I had been in evangelism for some time, it occurred to me that few, if any evangelists, were holding meetings on mission fields. We were sending all kinds of missionaries, other than evangelists. We were sending medical missionaries, educational missionaries, pastoral missionaries, construction missionaries and so on. That is no longer true. Many evangelists now travel to foreign lands and hold meetings. Anyway, I felt that the Lord wanted me to hold some such meetings, and for a number of years I preached in at least one foreign country each year. The Lord greatly blessed my meetings abroad. I do not remember ever giving an invitation abroad without people being saved.

One of the most fruitful fields I visited was the Bahama Islands. My first meeting there was at the invitation of my missionary friend, Rev. Robert Neighbour. He invited me to come to West End, Grand Bahama, and bring my tent and hold a meeting.

Following his suggestion, I went to considerable trouble and encountered some disappointment, but that trip proved to be one of the most exciting and fruitful I ever made.

I am sure Brother Neighbour had not had great experience with gospel tents, so he could not have anticipated what would be involved in getting the tent and equipment to the island. I had to load the tent, with all the poles, iron stakes, ropes, electric wire, lights, public address equipment, and seat ends on a two ton truck and haul it to West Palm Beach, Florida. From there, he told me we could ship the tent and equipment to West End on a small ship.

In due time, with all the equipment loaded on my truck, I left for West Palm Beach with eight or more of my church members, most of them traveling in a separate automobile.

Brother and Mrs. Neighbour preceded us to Florida and made arrangements for lodging for our party overnight. When we arrived, he told me that the boat had left early, and we would have to make other arrangements to ship the tent and equipment. Not having any idea what was involved, he thought we could ship the tent and equipment on the plane. I thought not. Nonetheless, the next morning we all arrived at the airport shortly before flight time in two cars and the truck.

At that time the only airline flying regularly scheduled flights from Florida to the Bahamas was Midet Airline, a small company that was flying DC-3 planes. The DC-3 was two-motor, prop-driven aircraft that seated twenty-one passengers.

It is impossible to describe the reaction of the people at Midet Airlines when ten or more adults, and three or four babies and children, showed up, almost late, with their luggage, boxes of groceries calculated to last a week, and all the junk we had in the truck. Saying that they were fit to be tied is putting it mildly.

When the baggage handlers looked in our truck and saw the tent, five big bags of it, wire, poles, stakes, lumber, PA system, recorder, podium, songbooks, iron seat ends, and other items too numerous to mention, they almost went into orbit.

The entire airline organization, from the president of the company to the people who loaded the plane, were in turmoil. They all threw up their hands in disbelief. There was no way they would fly all that load to West End on their airline. They didn't have that kind of cargo space.

After much discussion and head shaking, another person went out to take a look in the truck. It may have been the president of the company for all I know. It is a wonder he did not have a heart attack on the spot. He went back to his office shaking his head. We followed and waited while he talked it over with the rest of his people. There followed much more talking and much more shaking of heads.

Brother Neighbour should have been a diplomat. Somehow he pacified the airline people and persuaded them to take us and our baggage and equipment to West End, though they said they could not take the iron stakes. We would have to cut wood stakes on the island. And they could only take part of the tent this trip. They would have to bring the rest of the tent on the next flight, two days later.

Finally, with half of the tent and equipment, we were all loaded on the airplane and headed for the island. After a short overwater flight of eighty-five miles, the plane nosed down for a landing at West End. I looked out at the island and saw the runway, and a spontaneous prayer rose to my lips. "Lord, give me this island for Christ." I believed that He was going to do it.

After more than the usual hubbub of deplaning, collecting baggage, passing through customs, and getting transportation to the village, we reached a two story house Brother Neighbour had engaged for us to stay in.

With considerable effort we unloaded all we had brought with us. We stowed the part of the tent and equipment we had brought on a side porch. The rest of our paraphernalia we carried inside. Then I set forth to find a place to pitch the tent. Imagine my consternation when I found that the island was almost solid rock. There was no way we could drive wooden stakes in that ground. Greatly disappointed, I returned to the house.

It was now well past noon, and the ladies were stirring about in the groceries we had brought, trying to decide what to fix for our lunch. About that time one of the men came in with some fish he had bought from someone. I volunteered to clean the fish, and took them down to the seaside and started scaling them.

Soon a native lady approached me. "Are you a preacher?" she asked.

"Yes, I'm a preacher." I had no idea why she thought I was a preacher.

"What kind of preacher are you?"

"I'm a good preacher," I teased.

"I don't mean that. What denomination are you?"

"I'm a Baptist."

"Me too," she smiled. "Will you preach for us tonight?"

"Where will I preach?"

"In the lodge hall. Our church has services there."

"How will the people know I'm going to preach?"

"We'll tell them. You'll have a crowd. You'll see."

"All right. I'll be glad to preach for you."

That night the lodge hall was packed, and I started one of the greatest revivals I have ever had. We had people saved in every service. Often there were many professions. There was great excitement and much joy. Many testified of the great change that had come into their lives.

The last service was held at ten o'clock in the morning, the day we were to leave on the noon plane. That day the school dismissed their classes so the students could attend the last service of the meeting. The lodge hall was packed to overflowing. Great numbers of people filled the yard and lined the road.

After preaching, I gave the invitation. At once people started coming to the front and falling on their knees. Soon there was no more room at the front, so they started kneeling in the aisles. Soon there was no more room in the aisles. I looked out through the windows and saw people on their knees on all sides of the building. I cannot even guess how many people were converted that day. The following testimonies I recorded will give some idea of the results of the meeting.

One young man said, "I am happier than I ever was in all my life."

A lady said, "I have never had such joy in my heart."

Another said, "Thank you, thank you, thank you, thank you, for coming to our island to preach."

Another said, "We would like to keep you in our island forever."

An elderly man said, "This is the greatest thing that has come to this island in my lifetime."

Another said, "We have never had such meetings as these, and we feel that this is God's last warning to these islands."

A lady said, "It is going to make our island a little heaven on earth."

The islanders pointed out to me the one known thief at West End, making it clear that they had no respect for him. Soon after that I met him on the road, stopped him, and made an effort to win him to the Lord. He was not really interested, so I placed my hand on his shoulder and prayed for him. Later I was told that he said: "I like that Father Arnold. He met me in the middle of the road and blessed me."

On a subsequent visit, a year later, an old man saw me walking by the sea and called me to his side.

"I want to talk with you," he began when I reached him. This island is a different place since you were here last year. People used to be unhappy, but they are happy now. They have stopped swearing and started singing. Every day I hear them going about singing *Jesus Never Fails.*

I am different too. Before I was saved, I used to worry, but I don't anymore. I don't have a pension or Social Security, such as you have in the States, but the Lord is taking care of me.

He proceeded to tell me how he was living from his garden, his few chickens, gifts from friends, and the sale of conch shells to tourists.

His talk reminded me of the testimony of the Psalmist. *"I have been young, and now am old; yet have I not seen the righteous forsaken, nor his seed begging bread"* (Psalms 37:25).

His testimony inspired me to write the following poem.

God Will Supply

A gray old man lived all alone
Without a thing to call his own.
When someone asked how he got by,
"I trust in God," was his reply.

I once was young, I now am old.
God will supply, I've oft been told.
God will supply, He feeds the birds.
I've read it in His holy Word.

"But aren't you lonely?" someone asked.
"And don't you tire from all your tasks?"
"My God is near," was his reply.
"He meets all needs, so I'll get by."

"But what when summer's flowers fade,
And no one comes to give you aid?"
"God cares for me," was his reply.
"His Word can't fail, so I'll get by."

The following year, after a second visit to West End, I wrote: "Since our first campaign in the Bahamas last March, the work has continued to go steadily forward. You cannot long be on the island without meeting converts from the first meeting. The young man who drives one of the two taxicabs at West End was converted in the meeting. Girls who serve in the dining room at the hotel at Butler's Village, and the women who clean the rooms were converted. Men who run the fishing boats were converted. On every hand I met converts, all of them testifying of their conversions, and, at the slightest opportunity, telling of what God has done in their lives."

This is only a small accounting of all that God did in this one island. I returned again and again for additional meetings, and God always blessed with outstanding results.

One of the most unusual experiences I had in the Bahama Islands was the time I went to Water Key. It is interesting how I happened to go to this island.

Some of the natives either have a strong intuition or they are very sensitive to the leading of the Lord. I was made aware of this during my first trip to Grand Bahama. A man traveled thirty miles in a small sailboat, arriving on Grand Bahama the night the meeting started. He came to where we were staying to see me that night after the service.

"Today I was out fishing, and I suddenly felt that I should quit fishing and go home and dress and come to Grand Bahama," he began. "When I found the meeting going on tonight, I knew why I had to come."

I led him to the Lord that night.

After that, every time I went to Grand Bahama he showed up. And every time he asked me to go to his island, Water Key, and preach. Each time

I told him I would be glad to go, but he would always say, "No, I can't ask you to go. You would have to go in a small sailboat. The sea would be rough, and you would get wet and cold."

At last one day, he told me that he had arranged for me to go. I was to go to the other end of Grand Bahama by taxi. He had arranged for a larger sailboat to meet me there, and from that point, we would sail to Water Key in sheltered waters.

Rev. Roy Harrison, now deceased, was in our party at Grand Bahama on that occasion, and he volunteered to go with me to Water Key.

We traveled up the island, as planned, and from there we set sail with a crew of three or four men, including the one who had arranged the trip. We sailed all day on a calm, crystal-blue sea. Late in the afternoon, we saw a small hill that appeared to rise out of the sea, and the men started pointing and saying, "Water Key! See? Water Key! See?"

As we drew near we saw a small harbor, pressed against an island that sloped up from the sea. A great number of people were gathered along the shore.

"Why are all the people here?" I asked.

"They are here to meet you."

"How did they know I was coming?"

"They heard it on the radio."

Water Key, I soon learned, was one of the most primitive of the islands. There were no automobiles, no highways, no bicycles, and no electric-

ity on the island. But they did have battery-powered radios. That morning, before we left Grand
Bahama, someone had called the radio station at
Nassau, on New Providence Island, by radio telephone and told that I was going to Water Key.
The radio station had broadcast the message, and
the people on Water Key had heard it on their
battery-powered radios.

That day none of the men went out fishing,
though that was the way they made their livings.
Instead they waited all day for me to arrive.

Their 95-year-old pastor was also waiting to
meet me. Later he told me that I was the second
preacher to visit his church from the outside during his pastorate of 70 years.

We disembarked on one of the most beautiful
islands I have ever seen. A pathway, lined with
seashells, paved with sand, and shaded by tropical trees, led up from the sea. The natives took
our bags, camera, and recorder, leaving us nothing to carry. They led us along the path, past in-
tersecting paths, to a thatched hut. The old pastor came along.

"This is your motel," the man who had invited me explained as he led us inside. The hut
contained only a bed, a chair, and a dresser. I
learned later that a family had moved out so we
could stay in it.

The natives placed our equipment and bags
in the hut, then led us across the path to another
hut and motioned us into it. It contained only a
table and two chairs. Another family had moved

out so we would have a place to eat.

"What would you favor for your dinner?" my friend asked.

"Anything you have will be all right," I told him.

He then insisted that we go with him and some others while the meal was being prepared.

We walked with them and the pastor a quarter mile to the church. I have never seen people who were more proud of their church, though it was a modest frame building. They took me inside and showed me the pews and the pulpit, with two chairs and a podium. Then they took me out and showed me the church bell, mounted on a low post about three feet above the ground. The bell was cracked on one side, so it only clanked when they rang it. Later I was able to get a beautiful brass bell off a railroad train and ship it to them.

Back at our dining room, they served us fried Spam, pigeon peas, and maybe some fruit, though I'm not sure. We ate, went to our "motel," rested briefly, then dressed and started to church.

The paths were crowded with people, also going to church. The church was crowded when we arrived, and people kept pressing their way in until there was standing room only. Every person on the island, except one blind man, attended the service, I was told.

What a service we had! The people sang, as only they can sing. I preached. Brother Roy gave a brief testimony, and the pastor gave a brief message. The power of God was present. There was shouting. There was rejoicing, and people got saved.

The next morning, the people were up early. Someone cooked us a good breakfast. We ate it and thanked them. Then we went out and found that people were scouting all over the island, gathering up souvenirs for us to take back with us. While they were doing that, two of the men gave us a demonstration of how they hand-made rope from a tropical plant that they called a sisal.

Soon it was time to go, for we had a long journey back across the sea and down Grand Bahama to West End. The wind had changed, and we would have to cross to the other side of the island so we could board in calm water.

We told the people good-bye and started on our way. To my surprise, everyone, including the old pastor, walked with us. About a mile on the way, he excused himself, saying that he had not been feeling well for a few days, but the rest of the people continued with us.

We had been walking on level ground, but we soon went down into a kind of a natural amphitheater, bounded by tropical growth on ever side. There the people paused and started singing. We listened, enthralled. After the song, they asked that we preach to them. We preached, prayed, told them good-bye again and started on. They all continued with us to the sea.

There they sang again, and asked that we preach again. Once again I preached, prayed and told them good-bye. We got in the boat and thrust off as the people on the shore started singing, *God be with you till we meet again.* They were still singing when we sailed out of hearing. If they could have walked on the water, I believe they would have gone all the way to Grand Bahama with us.

On the Saturday before Christmas, Mrs. Arnold and I flew our Tri-Pacer plane to Bimini Island instead of going to our usual mission point at West End. I had never visited Bimini, and I wanted to assess the need for mission work there.

Early in the morning we took off from Fort Pierce and flew down the beautiful Florida coast to Fort Lauderdale. There we landed and refueled. Then we took off for Bimini, some sixty-five miles off the coast. I climbed the plane to 8,000 feet, so we would have considerable glide distance in case of engine failure. We watched the Florida coast fade in the distance behind us, and for a short time we were out of sight of land. That was the critical part of the flight, and we did not breathe easy until we saw the coast of Bimini dimly outlined in the distance.

In a matter of minutes we were gliding down to the runway for a landing on Bimini. We landed, got out of the plane and tied it down. The only way to get to the village was to ferry a short distance across an emerald-blue bay, so we caught the ferry.

We were hungry when we reached the village,

so we stopped for a bite to eat. While we were eating, we asked some native boys if there was a Baptist Church on the island.

"Yes there is. It's on the far end of the island. "Rev. Smith is the pastor," one of them said.

We finished eating, found lodging, and checked in. Then we walked up the island and found Pastor Smith's home.

He invited us in, and we sat down to talk of the Lord's work in the islands and especially of his work on Bimini.

"What kind of church do you have, Brother Smith?" I inquired.

"I have a good church," he replied. "I have 300 good members."

"What do you mean, good members?"

"I mean that they are good Christians. They do not drink. They do not gamble. They do not use bad language. They do not run around. Come to church tomorrow and you will see."

The next morning we arrived at the church in time to attend the most amazing Sunday school I have ever attended. The pastor made us welcome, and we sat with him while the superintendent conducted the opening part of the service.

All the people in attendance, except my wife and I, were of African ancestry. Their faces were dark, but they were radiant. The superintendent had the happiest, most radiant face I have ever seen. The glory of God seemed to radiate from him.

While he was conducting the service, an unusual thing happened. People suddenly broke into singing, *"O come, let us adore Him, O come, let us adore Him, O come, let us adore Him, Christ the Lord."* They did this over and over again throughout the Sunday school hour.

I had never heard a Christmas carol sung as they sung it. Each time they sang it, it rose higher and higher in praise and adoration until I wanted to prostrate myself at the feet of the precious Savior.

At one point the pastor leaned over and said, "The people are full of joy, because all this week we have been getting ready for Christmas.

"Each morning of this week, our people have come to the church at four o'clock to pray for an hour. Then they have gone home for breakfast and for the duties of the day. This morning they also came to church at four o'clock to pray for an hour. Then they went home for breakfast. Now they are back for Sunday school, and they are filled with the Spirit."

I felt that I was learning for the first time how to observe Christmas.

The church was packed for the morning preaching service. As in the Sunday school hour, the people again interrupted the service from time to time by singing, *"O come, let us adore Him."* They sung it with a spirit of reverence and worship, and though they interrupted the order of service, their singing never seemed out of order.

At one point the pastor whispered to me, "Do you notice that there are a few people seated on the two back pews?"

"Yes," I said, after noticing that those pews were not packed as were the others.

"Those pews are my goat pen," the pastor said.

I looked at him, puzzled, wondering what he meant.

"When any of our members are out of fellowship, they have to sit in the goat pen until they get right with the Lord and confess before the church. After that, they can again sit with the rest of the congregation."

Strangely that seemed to work for him. That morning after he preached, some of his wayward members came forward to make things right with the Lord and to get out of the goat pen. Others came forward for salvation.

Brother Smith preached a great sermon, but that is not what I remember about the service. To this hour, I cannot forget how the people sang, *"O come, let us adore Him. . . . Christ, the Lord."*

Both morning and evening, when the service ended, the people did not soon leave the building, nor did they begin to visit with each other. Instead they arose and stood in the aisles and around the walls of the auditorium, singing, *"O come, let us adore Him."*

I especially remember after I had preached that night, how they sang as they had in the morning. When they finally decided to go home, they sang as they left the building and turned homeward.

Little groups turned on different pathways,

still singing. I watched their flickering lights moving through the pines and palm trees, and I listened to patches of song, floating across the island from every direction, and gradually fading in the distance. *"O come, let us adore Him, . . . O come let us adore Him."*

The voices were at last lost in the distance, but, even after the passing of the years, their message of praise and worship remains strong in my memory.

Chapter 18

At Last an Evangelist

*F*rom the day I entered the ministry, I knew I was called to be an evangelist, but an older preacher told me that I ought to serve as a pastor for a time before entering the field of evangelism. "You will gain experience, and you will learn how to be a help to a pastor," he told me.

I took his advice and became a pastor, but I stayed in the pastorate longer than I planned. I enjoyed the pastorate, and God blessed me as a pastor. I loved my people, and I found that it was not easy to leave them. Besides, though the salary I received was small, it did provide a regular income. As an evangelist, I knew that I would have no certain income, that I would have to live by faith, and that I would have to be gone from home much of the time. But I knew God wanted me to be an evangelist, and during the years I served as a pastor, I also held every meeting I could.

During the years I was both pastoring and holding meetings, I was gaining valuable experience. I know now that the Lord was fashioning me for the work I was to do later in life.

In those years I went to hear every evangelist who held meetings within driving distance. I listened to them preach and watched them in action. I learned all I could from them, and their fires lighted my torch and helped to keep it burning.

The first books that fell into my hands after I started preaching were small paperback books of sermons by D. L. Moody. I read each one over and over. Other books of his sermons were then on sale by Moody Press for 25 cents per copy. Quarters were hard to come by, but every time I got a quarter I could spare, I ordered another book of Moody's sermons.

Later I read books by other men. A book by L. R. Scarbough, entitled, *With Christ After the Lost,* fired my soul. From that book, I learned much about winning people to Christ. R. A. Torrey's great book on the Holy Spirit showed me my need of God's anointing power. It caused me to search the Scriptures to learn more about the Holy Spirit and how He works through men. It drove me to my knees to pray for the power of God upon my ministry.

Later, a preacher friend told me about a set of twenty volumes of sermons by T. De Witt Talmage. Somehow I managed to scrape together the money to buy that set of books. Talmage preached on all kinds of subjects. Some of his sermons did nothing for me, but others were masterpieces. He was a master sermon builder, and he was eloquent beyond description. From him I learned much about how to prepare sermons.

I read books by many more men than I can mention here. I simply devoured books. Mostly I read books by great preachers of bygone days. Especially I read sermons by evangelists who had been greatly used. Through all the years of studying and praying, I knew I was preparing for the day when I would become an evangelist.

Finally the day came when I began to pray definitely about how and when I was to go into evangelism. Not long after that, I had occasion to be on the campus of Tennessee Temple University, along with many other pastors from across America. Services were being held in the Highland Park Baptist Church, and during the morning sessions, Dr. Lee Roberson conducted his daily radio broadcast from the platform. One morning while the broadcast was in progress, to my surprise, Dr. Roberson called me to the platform and proceeded to interview me over radio. It really threw me when he asked, "When are you going into evangelism full time?"

I had told no one that I was wrestling with that very question, so he had no way of knowing that I had been praying about it for weeks.

"I—I really don't know," I stammered, for I had not yet decided when I would.

Dr. Roberson then told me that I ought to go into evangelism and stay there for the rest of my life.

Soon after that I became convinced that the Lord wanted me to resign the church I had organized and built and step out into evangelism. I had no assurance that I would be invited for meetings, and I had no guarantee of an income, but I believed that the Lord would take care of me.

One Sunday morning not long after that, when I entered the auditorium of my church, I heard from Heaven. The Lord could not have spoken more clearly if He had sent me a telegram. The Lord told me that He wanted me to resign my church that day. That morning, at the close of the service, I called the men of the church together and told them that I was going to resign. I did not have my letter of resignation written, but I would write it that afternoon, and I would read it to the church that night.

Thirty days later, I preached my farewell sermon, told the people good-bye, and left the church. I was out of a job. I no longer had a salary, so I had to depend on the Lord to open doors for me and to meet my needs.

I left the pastorate in the spring of 1972. Doors started opening to me at once, and soon I was holding meetings in several states each year. Since I entered the field of evangelism full time, I have had many blessed revivals in churches from Florida to California, and from Mississippi to Massachusetts.

Many pastors have invited me to hold meetings in their churches again and again. God has blessed my meetings. I have seen the lost converted, backsliders reclaimed, Christians revitalized, and churches set aflame. Pastors often tell me that their churches experience healthy growth following my meetings.

I have missed pastoring, since I have been an evangelist. I have missed people who had become dear to me, but I have never regretted that I became an evangelist. After I had been in evangelism for a few years, a strong church with great potential wanted to call me to be their pastor. I wanted to take that church. My wife really wanted me to take it, but I waited and prayed. When the answer came, I knew that God wanted me to stay in evangelism. That settled it. I told the men of the church that, much as I would like to be their pastor, the Lord had told me to stay in evangelism. Enough time has now passed for me to look back and see that God's way was the best way.

For one thing, if I had taken on the responsibility of pastoring that church with its varied ministries, I would never have had time to write the books the Lord has led me to write. The pressures of evangelism are great, but I am able to make time to write. Writing has become a large part of my ministry.

True to my calling, I am still an evangelist. I continue to preach on radio every day, and I continue to travel and preach in revivals. I usually preach in thirty or more churches each year. In my meetings I kindle revival fires, call Christians to a closer walk with God, and lead the lost to receive Christ as Savior. Writing is an added ministry, but it does not keep me from continuing in my first calling.

My writing is now reaching people I will never see in this world, and the books I have written, and others I plan to write, will be in the world long after I have gone to my reward.

Chapter 19

Writing on the Front Burner

*M*y mother had a gift for writing, and I think she may have prayed that I would be a writer as well. If in Heaven she knows about the books I have written, I think she must rejoice.

I now know that the Lord intended for me to be a writer. The time came when I felt and answered the call to write, but I was writing long before that,

From childhood I had a yen to write. I used to make up stories and compose poems as I walked the mile to and from school. Walking seemed to stimulate my mind and often started me composing a story or a poem. I often put my thoughts on paper when I got to where I was going. One of the things I wrote on those daily walks was a poem entitled *The Schoolhouse in the Wood.*

I composed this poem and committed it to memory as I walked. Later I put it on paper and took it to our local newspaper editor. He published it in the Lancaster paper, *The Central Record.* It is hard to express how much the publication of that poem encouraged me. I am reprinting it here with some appropriate comments.

The Schoolhouse in the Wood

Between the crossroads once there stood,
  A one-roomed structure, plain and drear.
It was the schoolhouse of the wood,
  With mountains towering in the rear.
To grace the eyes, the wild rose grew
  Upon the mountain's jagged side,
And across a sky of blue,
  Like a golden ball, the sun did ride.

Part of the preceding verse was based on my imagination. I seemed to have plenty of imagination, even as a boy. The school I attended was not in the woods, and there were no mountains in the rear. My school was in the forks of the road, and rolling farmland was all around it. At the time I wrote this poem, I had never seen a mountain.

The next four verses of the poem were based upon my own experiences. Young as I was, I had an awareness of what I saw, and I had a memory for details.

Inside the room, since sharp at eight,
  The classes had gone forward slow,
For impatient students scarce could wait
  For recess, so they could go.
While waiting thus, they whispered some,
  And sometimes paper wads did throw,
And wish that soon the hour would come
  When they could march out row by row.

Some students to their books gave heed,
　As they were thus inclined.
But some would just pretend to read,
　While wondered far afield their mind.
Some made marks upon the wall,
　And some carved initials on their desks,
For the master could not watch them all,
　Though he did his very best.

Yet oft' the cruel lash would fall,
　When some transgressor had been found,
A warning and example to them all,
　That made them quietly settle down.
The minutes lengthened into hours;
　The sun was in the western sky.
The lengthening shadows formed like
　　towers,
　Reminding one of ages long gone by.

Then came the closing hour of school,
　And the students, standing row by row,
According to the master's rule
　Marched outside with footsteps slow.
Then turned upon the homeward road,
　With joyful shouts and happy play,
Sought each his home, a meek abode,
　In the cool of the dying day.

The next verse was taken partly from what I
had seen and partly from my imagination. Even
from my youth it appears that I had a strong
imagination. I used it often to write poems and

make up stories. I often wrote them on paper and
read them to my mother.

> The sky fast changed from blue to red;
> The shadows fell below;
> A familiar sound was heard o'er head,
> The lonely "caw" of a lonely crow.
> A smoldering fire, the sun's rim glowed,
> Through whispering pines on the
>   mountain's crest.
> And dazzling, changing colors flowed
> Across the sky from the golden west.

From this point on, the poem is written purely
from my imagination.

In the dying splendor, hand in hand,
  Two loitered on their way,
Enjoyed the fragrance of God's land,
  The closing of God's day.
A boy and girl, behind the rest,
  With spirits running high
With emotions they could not express,
  Forgot that night was drawing nigh.

'Twas Mary Allen, a maiden sweet,
  Just blooming into womanhood,
A graceful creature from head to feet,
  The tranquil beauty of the wood.
Like golden rod, her wavy hair.
  Her eyes were violet blue.
Her cheeks like roses, rich and rare,
  Her smile was winning, true.

And David Long, a slender lad,
　With eyes as blue as steel,
Loved Mary Allen, the only girl he'd had.
　And as they walked across the field,
He asked her if she would be his wife,
　When they were come of age.
She smiled and said, "I'll share your life,
　Until we reach the final page."

Now years have past; they have grown old.
　Together they have shared the years.
They've known the heat and the cold,
　The sunshine and the tears.
And now beside a new schoolhouse,
　They watch their grandchildren play—
And smiling through their tears rejoice
　That they have reached this day.

I now see the shortcomings of this poem I wrote as a child, and I consider it most kind that the editor printed it in our local newspaper.

Many of the things I wrote in those early days have been lost. Perhaps it is best that they were, but I am glad this poem survived.

I was ill prepared for the task of writing, but I started anyway. It was a kind of on the job training. Much of what I wrote in the beginning ended up in the trash can. I am glad, for that was where it belonged. Some articles and poems I submitted to magazines. Many of them brought only rejection slips. They named them right, and that is exactly how I felt, rejected. But I kept on writing, and finally one day a magazine accepted something I had written for publication. They paid me for it too—a whole dollar. That was the most appreciated dollar I ever earned. It meant that at last I was a paid, published writer.

After that I had more and more material accepted and paid for. Some of what I wrote appeared in leading religious publications. I really felt that I had arrived when something I wrote was published in a magazine that went into 104 countries of the world.

I finished writing my first inspirational novel, *The Legend of Old Faithful*, just before the outbreak of WWII. A lady who belonged to my church typed it for me, and I sent it off to a publisher. I had no idea that the manuscript needed to go through several revisions and be proofread several times before submitting it to a publisher.

I was greatly elated when someone from the publishing company wrote and told me that they were interested. (I now marvel that they were interested at all.) They wanted to submit the manuscript to another publisher they were working with, and, with my permission, they sent it off to them.

There followed anxious days of waiting. Then, to my great disappointment, I received a rejection letter. Because of the war and the resulting shortage of materials and manpower, they had decided not to undertake publishing my book.

Great as that disappointment was, I have lived to thank God for their decision. *The Legend of*

Old Faithful was not then ready for publication. Years later, after many revisions and rewrites, it was published. Had it been published in the beginning, it would not have been as good a book as it was when it finally went to press.

For many years, because of the pressures of a busy ministry, my writing was put on the back burner. Finally, in 1983, I decided that if I was ever going to write the books I believed the Lord wanted me to write, I had better begin writing in earnest.

Soon after that, some friends made it possible for me to buy a computer. I taught myself how to use it, and started using it to write. Since then, I have missed very few days writing,

Two years later I had a book on prophecy, *Israeli Countdown to Eternity*, published. One year after that my first novel, *The Legend of Old Faithful*, was published.

The books I have written have been far better received by the reading public than I ever expected. They have gone into every state and into several foreign countries. From the time when *The Legend of Old Faithful* was released until the present, letters have come from thousand of my readers, praising my books and urging me to keep on writing. Each year more and more people order the book I am working on as soon as I announce the title. For several years I have been numbering and autographing books that are ordered before publication, and each year the number of people who order before publication increases.

Another surprise has been seeing how my books sell themselves. For example, someone will borrow one of my books or get one from a library. After reading it, they frequently write to me or to one of my publishers, asking for lists of my other books so they can order them. I will be forever grateful to my loyal readers for making my writing ministry so successful, and, just as they have requested, I plan to keep on writing.

I have several books in my mind that I plan to write. I usually think about a story for two or more years before I write it. It is not unusual for me to have four or more books started, but I concentrate on one of them until it is finished.

I plan to keep on writing a book each year for as long as the Lord gives me the health and ability to do so.

Chapter 20
Things I've Seen God Do

*I*f I had no Bible, if I had never heard of God, I would still believe in Him. I have seen Him do too many wonderful things to ever doubt His existence. In my years of walking with God, I have seen some big miracles and more than my share of small miracles, many of them performed on my behalf. I trust that my account of them will strengthen the faith of my readers.

God Stopped the Rain

While I was doing mission work in Eastern Kentucky, a brother preacher and I started a broadcast on a radio station in Williamson, West Virginia. Soon there was so much interest, we started holding open-air services on Pond Creek, across the Kentucky line from Williamson. Good crowds attended from the beginning, and several people were converted.

For these services, we set up a pulpit in an open area, not far off the highway. We hooked up a loud speaker, and passed out hymnbooks to the people as they gathered for the service. I do not recall whether we had a musical instrument or not.

One afternoon, just as we started the service, there was a rumble of thunder and a rush of wind. Dark clouds swept across the sky. Big raindrops started splattering on the pavement and wetting the people, and there was a sudden rush as people started to leave.

I stepped to the microphone and said in a loud voice, "Just a minute. We are going to ask God to stop the rain until the service is over."

Most of the people stopped where they were while I prayed. At once the wind abated, and the clouds started moving away from us. We continued with the service and had good results.

As we were taking down our equipment, a man drove up in a thoroughly drenched automobile. "Didn't it rain here?" he asked, looking puzzled.

"We asked God to stop the rain, and He did," I told him.

"It washed everything away a half mile down the road," he declared, shaking his head in dismay.

About that time someone came from the other direction and told us that there had been a flood of rain a half mile up the road.

In the press of passing years, I had forgotten this event. Then on the day I was observing my fiftieth anniversary in the ministry, a man stood up during the opening exercise and told that he had been present the day God stopped the rain.

God Supplied Gas in An Emergency

Late one winter night, as I was returning home from Sunday services in the Belphrey Baptist Church, in Pike County, Kentucky, God performed a small miracle for me.

In the rush of that day, I had forgotten to fill my gas tank. I did not think of it until the motor of my car started missing as I was driving home. I glanced at the gas gauge and saw that it was on empty, so I guided the car to the roadside, and it rolled to a stop. I turned off the ignition and the lights, knowing that I was in trouble. It was about one o'clock in the morning; it was very dark, and it was bitter cold—about 15 below zero.

As my eyes grew accustomed to the darkness, I saw that my car had stopped beside a small gas station. There was an outside stairway leading up to an apartment above the station. Relieved, I climbed the stairway and rapped on the door.

"Who is it?" a man called.

"I'm a preacher, and I'm out of gas."

"Go away. I'm not going to get up and pump gas for you."

I begged and pleaded, but nothing I said made any difference. He simply was not going to come out and pump gas for me.

Finally, I went down the steps, stopped behind my car, and bowed my head in prayer. I told the Lord my situation, as if He did not already know. I apologized for not remembering to buy gas, and I told the Lord I really needed help.

When I raised my head and opened my eyes, I was amazed to see a tiny crack of light in the distance. That was strange, I thought, for I had not seen that light before. I moved my head an inch to the left, and the light disappeared. I moved back and saw the light again. I moved to the right and the light again disappeared. It was only visible from one position, and I had opened my eyes in that exact spot.

I started walking toward the light. It led me across the highway, then across some railroad tracks, and finally to a boxcar. Inside the boxcar some men were talking, so I called to them.

"Who is it?" one of them asked.

"I'm a preacher, and I'm out of gas."

"That's no problem. We have a fifty gallon drum of gas," he called back.

A moment later he opened the door and came out. "I'll get you some gas," he said as he led me along the tracks to a flat car. He got a five gallon can and filled it from the drum he had mentioned. Then he went with me to my car and poured the gas in the tank. He refused to let me pay him, so I thanked him. He waited until I started the car. I waved good-bye to him and started home, thanking God for answered prayer.

Gas In a Rainstorm

Some years later, I was driving home from a

broadcast on the Winchester radio station, about eighteen miles from Lexington. On the way, I was caught in an unusually hard rainstorm. About that time my motor sputtered, and I realized that I had forgotten to refill the gas tank. A glance at the gauge confirmed that I was out of gas.

I guided the car out of the road and it stopped on a grassy shoulder. I looked out the window at the pouring rain and started praying. I told the Lord it was my fault that I had run out of gasoline, and I was sorry. I also told Him that I didn't mind walking after gas, but that it was raining. I would get wet if I walked in the rain, and I would likely get a cold. That would make me sound terrible on the radio. I asked the Lord to either stop the rain or send me some gasoline.

A moment later, a pickup truck stopped beside my car. The man in the truck rolled down his window, and I rolled down my window.

"Why, Preacher, I almost didn't recognize your car in all this rain," he said. "What's your trouble?"

"I'm out of gas," I replied, wondering who he was and how he had recognized my car. I did not remember having seen him before.

"I just happen to have some gas. Don't get out of your car and get wet. I'm wearing a raincoat, and I'll put the gas in your car."

He parked in front of me, got a five gallon can of gas from the back of his pickup, and poured it in my gas tank.

"What do I owe you?" I asked as he came to

my window.

"Not a thing. The Lord sent you that gas. This morning as I started to leave home, I had a sudden impression that I ought to go to the garage and get the five gallon can of gas I had there and bring it with me. I had no idea why, but I know now. The Lord knew you were going to run of gas, so He told me to bring that can of gas." Somewhat amazed, I thanked him. I thanked the Lord as I was driving on to Lexington.

Oil On a Mountain

Some years ago, one of the men in my church and I drove my pickup truck to Florida. On our way home, the motor started missing badly. A mechanic told us that the motor appeared to have a cracked piston. He thought I could drive home before getting it repaired, though it would probably use a lot of oil.

My friend and I wanted to get home, so we decided to drive the truck as it was. The mechanic proved to be right about it using oil. We had to add oil every few miles. I finally bought a case of oil, thinking that would be enough to take us the rest of the way home. But the condition of the motor worsened, and it started using even more oil.

In Tennessee, on Jellico Mountain, I poured the last quart of oil we had in the motor. Before we reached the top of the mountain, the oil pressure dropped again, so I pulled the truck to the side of the road and stopped, knowing that we were miles from a gas station.

"What do we do now?" my friend asked.

"First we pray," I replied. Then I bowed my head and asked the Lord to send help.

Minutes later a run-down old jalopy of a car stopped. "Are you broke down?" a man asked.

"Low on oil. My truck is throwing it out."

"My car wastes oil too, so I carry a case with me all the time." He got two quarts of oil from the trunk of his car and brought them to me. "This ought to last 'til you get to Jellico where you can buy oil. It's down the hill most the way from here."

He refused pay, so we thanked him. Then we thanked the Lord and poured the oil in the crankcase of the truck and started on. In Jellico we bought enough oil to last the rest of the way home.

Jumper Cables in a Hurry

I was running late on my way to a revival in Ohio. About a hundred miles from the church, I pulled into a rest area and turned off the ignition. When I returned a few minutes later, the battery was down, and the motor would not start. I reminded the Lord that I was running late and asked Him to send help. Then I raised the hood of my car and stood by it waiting.

In a few minutes a car, pulling a U-haul trailer, came in on the other side of the median, parked, got out and looked my way. He got back in his car, did a U-turn in the parking area, drove the wrong way to the end of the median, then turned, and drove to where I was parked.

"What's your trouble?" he called as he stopped.

"My battery is down."

"I have jumper cables. I'll start you."

He started my car, drove out of the rest area and hurried on his way, as if he had only stopped to help me.

I thanked the Lord and continued on to my meeting.

Preservation on the Highway

When one drives the highways as much as I do, there have to be some close calls. The way I was delivered from some of them makes them qualify as miracles. One night, driving home from a meeting in a church in the Knob section of Kentucky, I had such an experience.

It started snowing before I reached the church that night, and by the time the service was over, there was an inch or more of snow on the ground. I did not mind driving in the snow, but I was concerned about getting over the steep knob on the narrow, country road.

To my great relief, though the car did considerable skidding on the way up the knob, I reached the top without mishap. The road was much steeper going down the other side, so I applied pressure on the brake pedal before starting down. My intention was to ease the car down the hill slowly, but it did not work out that way. Instead, the brakes locked, and the car started skidding down the hill like a runaway sleigh. I had to fight the steering wheel to keep the car on the narrow road.

The last hundred yards of the hill were almost straight down, and the road made a sharp turn to the left at the bottom. On that stretch of road, the car gained speed, and I had to fight even harder to keep it in the road. I was sure I could not make the curve at the bottom of the hill. Only a miracle would keep the car from leaving the road and crashing down an embankment into the trees. I continued to pray as the car approached that curve.

Then something miraculous happened. At the foot of the hill, the car suddenly slowed. It went around the curve without the slightest skid and stopped. I took time to thank the Lord before I started on.

A similar thing happened one day when I was driving in the mountains. There was a glaze of ice on the highway, and on the way down a mountain my car spun out of control. It continued down the mountain, spinning like a top, only much slower. There was nothing I could do but pray.

The car finally stopped spinning and headed straight toward the shoulder of the road and a drop of several hundred feet. There was no guardrail to stop me, so I prayed, "Lord save me."

The front wheels of the car dropped over the shoulder of the road, and the car stopped. God had become my guardrail.

I had another close call on a snow-covered road while I was pastor of Liberty Baptist Church in Garrard County, Kentucky. I left the church in the afternoon to drive to Lancaster. On the way I topped a hill and started down the other side. At the foot of the hill, a stalled car had been left on a bridge. There was room for one car to pass between the stalled car and the concrete railing of the bridge, but there was not room for two cars.

As I approached the stalled car, a car, coming to meet me, was picking up speed before starting up the slick hill. By the time he saw my car, he was coming too fast to stop on the slick road. His car reached the rear fender of the stalled car just as my car reached the front finder. I saw no way we could avoid a head-on crash. All I could do was send a prayer heavenward.

Then a marvelous thing happened. The approaching car skidded to my left, and my car skidded to my right. Then it appeared that the sides of the cars would collide. At that instant, both cars started skidding in the opposite directions. My car cleared the back finder of the stalled car by an inch. The other driver must have come that near hitting the railing of the bridge. Neither car got a scratch.

I was so shaken by what had happened, I decided I must have underestimated the space between the stalled car and the bridge. Just to make sure, I went back, and measured the space. Sure enough, there was not room for two cars to pass. But they had passed! Only God could have made that happen.

Lest this chapter grow too long, I will relate only one more account of close calls while driving. I doubt that I was in great danger of an injury in this one, but my car would certainly have been greatly damaged.

While on my way to a church in Louisville, Kentucky, I stopped my car before turning on a cross street. I waited for a car that was approaching from my right to clear the intersection. The driver attempted to turn left onto the street where I had stopped, but he turned too short, and his car headed straight toward the front of my car. I braced for the impact, but just at that instant, a car, traveling at a good rate of speed, came down the cross street from my left. It struck the rear bumper of the car that was about to crash into my car. It spun the car around, causing it to miss my car and go across the road where it hit a utility pole and stopped. Both cars were damaged, but no one was injured.. I drove away without a scratch and without being made late for church that night because of an accident.

Chapter 21

I Know God Is Real

Just to Make the Devil Shut up

*O*ne day as I was driving to Winchester, Kentucky, to conduct my daily broadcast, the devil got in the car and rode with me. I hadn't invited him, but he rode along anyway. The minute I started, the devil began talking to me. Of course, I didn't see the devil, but I knew he was there. I didn't hear his voice, but that didn't keep him from talking to me.

"You are a big fool," he began. "Think how much money you are going to owe for the broadcasts on all the stations you are on. People won't send in enough money to pay for the station time, and you'll go broke trying to pay for it. Besides, think of that big church you're building! All of your church members will go broke trying to pay for it. A depression is coming, and you'll never get out of debt."

I don't usually do anything like I did that day, but the devil doesn't usually talk to me the way he did that day either. If I had let him get by with what he was saying, I would never have heard the last of it. I would not advise anyone else to do what I did, but I felt that the Lord wanted me to do it.

Instead of answering the devil, I started talking to the Lord. I told the Lord that I wanted Him to make the devil shut up, and I asked Him to do something special that would do it.

"Lord, when I get to Winchester, I'm going to turn on Main Street and park in the nearest parking place," I prayed. "Then I'm going to walk to the nearest street corner and stand there for five minutes by my watch. I'm not going to speak to anyone unless they speak to me first. While I am standing there, I want you to send me enough money to pay for one broadcast on the Winchester station."

When I reached Winchester, I turned on Main Street and parked my car in the first open parking place. I got out and walked to the nearest street corner, looked at my watch and stood there waiting.

In a couple of minutes a man came past. He recognized me, spoke briefly, handed me some money for the broadcast and went on. I counted the money. It was not enough to pay for a broadcast, and I told the Lord it was not enough.

"The devil will always say it just happened that the man was passing and gave me some money. So You had better hurry and send me the rest of the money before the five minutes is up."

About that time a lady walked past, then turned and came back. "Why, Brother Arnold, I

198

didn't expect to see you," she said. "I'm in a hurry, but I want to give you this for your broadcast." She handed me some bills and some change, then hurried on.

I looked at my watch, and it was coming up on five minutes. I counted the money in my hand, and it was exactly enough to pay for one day's broadcast on the Winchester radio station. Now for some reason, that station charged an odd amount for a broadcast. It was so many dollars and sixty cents. The Lord sent me the right amount of dollars and the sixty cents. Standing there on the street corner, with the money in my hand, I said, "Now, devil, you shut up. My God is big enough to take care of me."

Driving the Governor's Car

This is an account of how God provided in an emergency on a never-to-be forgotten trip to the beautiful country of Guatemala. The plane I had boarded for Guatemala stopped briefly in Mexico City, then took off for Guatemala. On the way, we flew over country that was stark, rugged, and rock covered, and we flew over beautiful mountains and wooded valleys. At length we landed in Guatemala City, and I got off with a movie camera and a broadcast quality, reel to reel, tape recorder—one of the first ones on the market.

I found that I was in one of the most beautiful and exciting countries I had ever seen. Called *The*

Land of Eternal Spring, the country was like a flower garden, with multicolored flowers blossoming in profusion everywhere. And there were birds of every hue. There were parrots, almost tame, in the shrubs and trees, small green ones, larger double yellowheads, and others. In the airport terminal, I had seen tame giant macaws with bright red, yellow and blue plumage, but I had not expected to see so many birds in the wild.

There were people everywhere, people of Indian descent, of Spanish descent, and some of other origins. They walked; they rode on burros, in carts, and in automobiles. They were exuberant, friendly, even playful. My heart ached for the opportunity to preach to them, and I was glad that my missionary friend, Robert Neighbour, had made arrangements for me to preach in some churches and missions while I was there.

When I arrived at the mission house, I found that the Neighbours had some sick babies. The Humes family, who were working with them, also had two sick babies.

By the time the meetings they had planned for me were over, the babies had grown worse, so both families felt that they should return to the States with me so the sick babies could receive the necessary medical care. But there was a problem. The missionaries did not have enough money to pay all their fares to Miami, certainly not enough to travel all the way home. The Humes family had been supported on the field entirely by one church, and that church had stopped sending their support. So they were entirely without money. The Neighbours had only limited funds, and I had not brought a great deal of money with me.

Brother Neighbour called the airline office and asked the price of the tickets to Miami. Then we made a careful accounting of the money we all had. We had enough to pay for the tickets, but there would be little left over. We would have to trust the Lord to get us home from Miami.

After an overnight flight, we landed in Miami and got through customs in time for breakfast. The Neighbours had enough money to buy their breakfast. I had enough to pay for breakfast for the Humes family and myself, with some left over. While we were eating, we discussed what we should do.

The Neighbours decided that they would stay with friends in Miami for a few days. I needed to go on to Lexington, and the Humes needed to go to their home in Louisville.

After we finished eating, we found a secluded place where we could pray. We explained our problems to the Lord, as if He did not already know about it. We asked Him to take care of the need. Then we returned to the waiting room to wait and see what the Lord would do.

In a few minutes, Brother Humes went off and sat down alone. A moment later a stranger sat down beside him. Then, just as if he had been asked, the stranger made a startling statement.

"You know," he said, "there's a company here

that is trying to find drivers to take some cars north to their owners. They will fill the tank with gas and pay $10.00 in cash to anyone with a driver's license who will drive a car north and deliver it to the owner."

It did not take long for Brother Humes to report this to the rest of us. We investigated and found that we could indeed get a car to drive home. We decided that with the tank full of gas, and the $10.00 from the company, and the money I had left, we could drive the car as far as Lexington, where I could get money for the Humes family to finish the trip to Louisville. We would just have to go light on food on the trip.

We found our way to the company with the cars and signed the necessary papers. They brought out an almost new car that belonged to the Governor of Illinois. They filled the tank with gas, gave us $10.00 in cash and handed us the keys.

We loaded our bags in the car and climbed in, thankful that the Lord had answered our prayers and had made it possible for us to go home in style and comfort.

A Fearful Night

A group of us were on our way back from a tour of several countries, including the Holy Land. In those days the airlines were still flying four-motor, propeller driven planes, so overseas trips were much slower and much more hazardous than they are today.

On this, my second trip to the Holy Land, we spent four weeks visiting Ireland, England, France, Italy, Greece, Egypt, Syria, Lebanon, Jordan and Israel. Several of my good friends traveled with me, including Dr. B. R. Lakin, nationally known evangelist, and Dr. Dallas Billington, pastor of the large Akron Baptist Temple, of Akron, Ohio.

At the end of the tour, we boarded a plane at Lod Airport in Israel for the flight to New York. The plane stopped in Rome, and we had a layover of an hour or more while the plane was made ready for the flight across the North Atlantic, by way of the Azores.

I was so exhausted from the days and nights of travel, I fell asleep soon after we took off from Rome. I must have slept for several hours, for I do not remember stopping to refuel again in Lisbon.

Hours later, Dr. Lakin reached across the aisle and shook me. "Wake up! Wake up!" he insisted. "We're in trouble. We were suppose to land in the Azores to refuel, but the airport was weathered in. We flew all the way back to Portugal to land, but the field there was also weathered in."

I saw that Dr. Lakin was really worried.

"The captain has not told us a thing. We do not know how much fuel we have. We may have to ditch in the ocean any minute," he continued with mounting anxiety.

I looked around the cabin of the plane and

saw that all the passengers were awake, and that most of them looked worried. Many, especially those in our group, were praying. Some of the others were talking in low anxious voices.

"This is serious," Dr. Lakin repeated. "We may have to ditch. We could all die."

For a moment I felt fear creeping into my heart, and I started praying quietly.

"Lord, we need help. We came on this trip to study, so we might be better prepared to do your work. Lord, many of those on this plane are Christians. Among them are some of your choicest servants. We want to get back to America to continue the work You have called us to do. I pray You will enable the pilot to make a safe landing."

Instantly, there came to my heart a feeling of peace, and I felt that the Lord was assuring me that we would land safely. I thought of the night the Apostle Paul stood on the deck of a storm-tossed ship and prayed. I remembered that the next morning he reported to those on board that a man had stood by him in the night and told him that the ship would be lost but that all on board would reach land safely. The Lord had spoken to me just as definitely, though in a different way. I closed my eyes and soon went back to sleep.

It was daylight when Dr. Lakin shook me awake again. "They are bringing us in on radar," he reported. "We are going to land at a military base on an island somewhere in the Atlantic."

A plane landing by radar was almost unheard of in that day. It was certainly not the routine procedure that we know today. We could crash, trying to land. I remembered the assurance the Lord had given me and relaxed.

I looked out the window of the plane and saw nothing but fog. It looked like a white mist. Moments later, I saw whiffs of mist swirling around the tips of the wings. Then we broke out of the clouds 300 feet above the runway of a United States Army Base. Our plane glided down, and the wheels bumped the runway. The worried passengers cheered and applauded.

We deplaned and were ushered into an army building where they served us a good, hot breakfast. They refueled our plane, and we soon took off for the rest of our flight across the North Atlantic.

I can never forget how thankful I was that the Lord heard the cry of His child that dark night. It was so wonderful to know the quiet peace that came into my heart. I had read in the Bible, ". . . *call upon me in the day of trouble: I will deliver thee, and thou shalt glorify me*" (Psa. 50:15). I called, the Lord delivered, and I was thankful.

Chapter 22
Unforgettable Events

Horse Ride at Night

When I arose at my home in Ashland, Kentucky, on a beautiful spring morning, I had no way of knowing that when night came I would find myself riding a huge workhorse, still wearing his harness, through a dark woods in the rain. Nor could I know that the silent stranger riding beside me would make a startling, and potentially dangerous, revelation concerning himself before the journey ended.

Early that morning I left home, picked up some preachers, and started to South Central Kentucky to participate in an area-wide revival. We drove to Lancaster and stopped at the home of Pastor Roy Gabbard, the coordinator of the meetings.

Brother Gabbard gave us a warm reception, and we sat down and talked for awhile. Then he turned to me and said, "Brother Arnold, since you have the car, I suggest that you drop this man in the first town and the next man in the next town and the next man in the next town, and so on. You take the last church down the road."

I realized that not only was I being sent to the last place down the road, but most likely it would be the place with the least opportunity.

By the time I delivered the preachers to the towns where they were to preach, the sky had become overcast, and it looked as if it were going to rain. With some trepidation, I drove to the next town. Then, following the directions Brother Gabbard had given me, I turned onto a gravel road. I followed it for a few miles, watching for a dirt lane that turned off to the right.

When I found the lane, I discovered that recent rains had turned it into a deeply-rutted mud lane. With sinking heart, I turned on the lane. In one place, a small wooden culvert that had been built over a stream had slipped out of the road. I had to get out and put it back in the road before I could go on. That is the only time I ever had to put a bridge across a stream before continuing a journey.

The mud lane meandered across fields and through a deep woods. At last I came out of the woods and found a house, the only one I had seen since leaving the gravel road. I stopped my car, got out, went to the door, and rapped. Shortly, a man opened the door and looked at me over the top of his glasses.

"I am the preacher," I greeted.

"What preacher?" he asked, looking puzzled.

"I came to hold a revival. Aren't you people expecting a revival?"

"Not as I know anything about," he replied.

"Thank you," I said. "I'll be on my way."

"No," he countered. "Since you're here, you might as well stay. While the old woman is gettin' supper, I'll send the kids around to tell the neighbors, and we'll have a service."

"There is a church nearby?" I questioned.

"Yeah, we got a church."

Just then it started drizzling rain. I knew the rain would make the muddy lane even worse than it was already, and I started wondering how I would get my car back to the road. About that time a man rode up on a huge workhorse. He was leading another equally large workhorse. Both horses had harness on them.

"Come on in," my host invited, holding the screen door open.

"I had better get my car back to the road before the lane gets impassible," I told him.

I turned to the man on the horse. "Will you follow me out to the road with your team?" I asked. "I'll leave my car in somebody's barn lot, and I'll ride back on the horse you're leading."

He nodded that he would.

"I'll be back before long," I told the man in the doorway, as I started back to my car.

It was a good thing the man followed me with the horses, because I got stuck in the mud at least twice, and he had to pull me out. It was almost dark by the time we reached the road, and I found a place to park my car.

By the time I got the car parked, mounted the horse, and we started back, I could not see the road, but the horses knew their way. I can still hear the sound of the horses' hooves on that muddy lane, and I still remember how the mud splattered on me. I could not see the man riding beside me, but from time to time I could feel him brush against me when the horses got too close together.

I attempted to engage him in conversation, but he would not talk. He would not even answer questions I directed at him. At length I gave up, and we rode on in silence.

We soon reached the darkest part of the woods. I could see nothing, not a star in the sky, not the silhouette of a tree, not even the shadow of the man and the big horse beside me.

I became aware of the sounds of the night, the muffled sloshing of the horses' hooves, the clanking of the harness chains, and the croaking of small frogs in a nearby stream. Suddenly my companion broke his silence.

"I just got out of the asylum yesterday," he stated.

I could feel the hair rising on my head. Fervently, I hoped they had not let him out too soon.

He said no more. Apparently he was content with that simple statement.

The rain continued to fall in a slow drizzle. I could feel the cold wet drops pelting my face. Then I saw a light ahead, that signaled the end of our journey. I breathed a sigh of relief. I would soon be out of the dark and the rain, and away from danger—if there was any.

I soon sat down to a good meal with the family that had made me welcome. After we finished eating, the family got ready to go to church. Then my host brought out an old kerosene lantern and lit it, and we stepped out into the dark, rainy night, with only the lantern to light our way.

When we reached the church, there were no more than a dozen people present. There was no one there to play the ancient piano, so we sang a song or two without it. I attempted to preach, but no one paid any attention to what I was saying. Most of those present appeared to sleep. One man played with a large, gold watch chain until the end of the service.

It was evident that they were not interested in having a revival. I learned that the church building was soon to be demolished because of a hydroelectric dam that was being built in the area. All the people were going to move away, because their houses were going to be torn down also. I thanked them for coming and told them that this was the end of the meeting.

The next morning I walked out to my car and started home. Brother Gabbard had told me that he was going to hold a meeting in a country church, near a town where I had dropped one of the preachers, so I stopped to see him on my way. I was embarrassed to tell him of my failure, but he was relieved.

The night before he had preached to a large crowd. It looked as if they were going to have a good meeting, but, because of a death in his church family, he had to go home. So he wanted me to stay and take the meeting. He would preach that night before leaving for home, and he would introduce me to the people. I agreed to stay and finish the meeting for him.

There was a good crowd that night. Brother Gabbard was a good preacher, and he preached a great sermon. At the end of the service, he told the people that he was leaving, and that I was going to take over the meeting. Their disappointment was evident. I was a young preacher, and I probably did not look like much of a preacher to them.

Despite the disappointment, a good crowd came to the ten o'clock service the next morning. The power of God was upon the service from its beginning. While we were yet singing, a young woman started weeping, and deep conviction settled upon the congregation. I stopped the song and called for an invitation hymn. A number of people, including the young woman, responded to the invitation at once. I did not even preach that morning.

During the rest of the week, we had a blessed revival, and I made some lifelong friends. Some of them were later to help me in organizing and building a number of churches.

From that experience I learned that we should never say anything is bad until God has finished with it, for He often turns failure into success. I have always been thankful for that lonely horse ride on a dark, rainy night because of the good meeting that followed.

Invaded by KKK

In 1947 I flew my plane to Knoxville, Tennessee, for a revival in the Pleasant Hill Baptist Church, four miles from Lenior City. Pastor G.R. Reynolds met me at the airport and drove me to where I was to stay.

Brother Emmett Griffin, a blind musician, who was a student at Tennessee Temple College (now a university), played the piano for the congregational singing and sang solos each evening. He was quite an attraction and helped to draw overflow crowds.

The meeting was better than average, but that would not have made a strong impression on my memory, for the Lord was giving me better than average meetings everywhere I went. But something did happen one night during that meeting that I have never forgotten.

That night, as we were getting ready to start the service, the pastor whispered and told me that the Ku Klux Klan was coming to the service.

I scarcely knew what to do. I had never had the Klan attend a revival service before, so I did not know what to expect. I had been told that sometimes Klan members attended revivals, wearing their hoods and robes, but that they usually did not disturb the services. They had been known to march past the offering plates at the front of the church, with each man placing a

$5.00 bill in the plate. If they did come tonight, I thought that would not be a bad idea, but I would much rather for them not to come. I did not know a great deal about the Klan, but I had heard that they were against black people, so I did not want to be involved with them. If they did come, I decided I would ignore them and preach the gospel as usual.

When the time came to start the service, the Klan had not made an appearance. I breathed a bit easier, thinking that perhaps they would not come, but I kept looking at the seats that someone had reserved for them in the center section of the church.

About halfway through the song service there was a stir about the door, and about 20 men, wearing white robes and hoods, filed in and seated themselves in the reserve section. The people already in the church did not react openly, yet I could feel tension in the atmosphere.

Soon one of the hooded men arose, walked to the front of the church, interrupted the service, and made a short speech. The content of the speech must have been bland, for I remember nothing he said. After he returned to his seat, the service continued.

When the time came for me to preach, I preached the gospel to everyone, including those in the Klan. None of the Klan members responded in any way. I thought perhaps their commitment to the Klan precluded their response to the gospel. At any rate, I was glad that I did not belong to an organization that causes a man to hide his identity behind a robe and a hood.

Someone made a picture of the Klansmen and gave me a copy. I still have the picture. It serves only to remind me of a meeting I held long ago. I am not interested in a hood and robe in this world. I am looking forward to a robe and a crown in the world to come.

A Funny Thing Along the Way

This is the story of a pastoral call that gave me something to chuckle about. Years ago, during my days as a pastor, I made a call in a home where the wife and the children were Christians, but the husband was an open sinner. He was involved in chicken fighting. He was not above using bad language, and he was frequently intoxicated. I had often tried to win him to Christ, but had not been successful, though he was fond of me and always appeared glad to see me.

He was often away from home, but one evening when I called on the family, I found him there. He had been drinking, and had imbibed enough to make him overly friendly and talkative. He monopolized the conversations, and he kept patting me on the shoulder and telling me how much he liked me.

At last I decided it was useless to try to talk to the other members of the family, so I turned to him. "Get on your knees, my friend. I'm going to pray for you," I told him.

Without hesitation, he got on his knees, and I knelt beside him and put my arm around him.

"Now, Lord I want to pray for this man. Of course, Lord you know he is drunk . . ."

"No I'm not Lord," he interrupted.

Perhaps he thought the Lord wouldn't notice that he was drinking if I didn't tell on him.

The Craziest Thing I Ever Did

A man shook me awake in the early dawn of Sunday morning as the train I was riding pulled into the station in Detroit. The day before, without knowing why, I had boarded a train for Detroit from Lexington, Kentucky. I had ridden the rest of the day and all night in a day coach. Past midnight, I had finally fallen asleep.

I rubbed the sleep from my eyes, realizing where I was and remembering that I did not know why I was there. I did not know one person in Detroit, though I had once talked briefly with J. Frank Norris, pastor of Temple Baptist Church in that city. He probably did not remember me, and I doubted that he would be in the city, since he did not live there and did not preach there on a regular basis.

The day before I had been busy with plans for Sunday services in the church I pastored, but I was stopped short by a strong impression that I should catch the noon train and go to Detroit. The impression made no sense to me. My people would be expecting me to be in my pulpit the next day, and I had no good reason for not being there. Besides, I could ill afford a trip to Detroit. I tried to dismiss the idea of going, but the impression grew stronger. Finally I decided that the Lord must be telling me to go, even though it made no sense to me.

I told the Lord that I was supposed to preach in my church the next day, but the impression only grew stronger. At last, I told the Lord that I would call one preacher I knew and see if he could fill my pulpit. If he could, I would go. Half hoping that the preacher could not fill my pulpit, I phoned him. He said he would be glad to preach for me, so I had run out of excuses. I dressed hurriedly, packed a suitcase, and rushed to the station in time to buy a ticket and board the train.

The man who had awakened me was extending his hand. "My name is Sam Jesse, I am pastor of a independent Baptist church in Burton, Kansas," he said.

"I am Louis Arnold. I pastor the South Elkhorn Baptist Church near Lexington, Kentucky," I responded, taking his hand.

"I suppose you have come to the fellowship meeting," he continued.

"I certainly have. Where is it?" I laughed, relieved.

"Temple Baptist Church, where Dr. Frank Norris is pastor.

"Dr. Norris will be there, and preachers will be coming from all over America. I hope you are going to stay all week."

I told Brother Jesse that I probably could not afford to stay that long.

"The church will feed us, and they will put us up in the homes of members," he assured me.

"Then I'll stay," I told him.

By that time the train was screeching to a stop at the station. So we collected our bags, and a moment later we got off the train. Some men were watching the passengers as they got off, and two of them approached us.

"Are you preachers?" they asked.

We pled guilty.

"Then come with us, and we'll take you to the church," they told us.

When we reached the church, they took us to the dining room, where breakfast was soon to be served. What a welcome we received. Preachers were shaking hands, talking, getting acquainted, and having a good time.

Soon we were served a good southern breakfast, even though we were in the North. I still remember the hot biscuits, bacon, eggs and coffee they served. After breakfast they registered us and assigned us to the homes where we were to stay.

When it was almost time for Sunday school, we preachers crossed the street to the auditorium of the Temple Baptist Church. There I attended the largest Sunday school class I had ever seen. I believe there were about two thousand adults in that class, including the preachers who had arrived early for the fellowship meeting. Dr. G. B.

Vick taught the class, and it was a blessing to hear him.

I can never forget the service that followed. Many memories, bright after all these years, come crowding into my mind—the great crowd that packed the huge auditorium—Dr. Norris' commanding appearance—Brother Fred Donelson and family, and Mother Sweet, missionaries who had recently escaped from Communist China— Dr. Norris' exceeding tenderness, as he brought them to the platform and presented them to the great audience—the sermons Dr. Norris preached, and the invitations he gave. And the response! I had never seen so many people saved in one service. More than 70 people confessed faith in Christ in the morning service.

I was overwhelmed. Dr. Norris had preached a good sermon, but I did not think it had been that great. The invitation he had given seemed almost indifferent to me, yet more than 70 people had gone forward to confess faith in Christ.

The service that night was a repeat performance—a good sermon—though not great, a poor invitation, and more than 30 people went forward to profess salvation. Again I was amazed. I had never seen such results.

That night I went home with the church family I was to stay with. I could hardly wait until I was seated in the living room with my host so I could ask him the questions that were burning in my mind.

"Do you have people saved in your church

every Sunday?" I asked as soon as we were seated. He told me that the numbers were not always as great, but that they did indeed have people saved in numbers every Sunday.

"How do you do it?" was my second question.

My host's reply contained the greatest one-line sermon I have ever heard.

"I will take myself as an example," he began. Here is his sermon: "I work for Ford Motor Company to pay expenses, but my business is serving the Lord."

That's it. That ought to be the business of every Christian. That was like Paul saying, *"For me to live is Christ."*

My host continued, "There are hundreds of others in our church just like me. They work in various places, but their business is serving the Lord.

"In our church, every night except Sunday night and Wednesday night, some group meets for prayer. Then they go out two by two, from door to door, soul-winning. When souls are saved, they follow up and get them in church the following Sunday if at all possible. They usually sit with them and walk the aisle with them when the invitation is given. That is how we do it."

During that fellowship meeting, I learned more about how to win souls and how to build a church than I had learned before or since. That week changed my life and my ministry. To this day, I thank God that I was willing to do something that looked crazy, once I was sure that it was what the Lord wanted me to do.

Behind Barbed Wire

We sat in our car looking out at the armed men who surrounded us. Beyond them were swirls of barbed wire, and there were more guards at the gate. We were imprisoned.

In the car with me were Dr. Dallas Billington, our driver, an armed guard, and Emil, our Christian Arab guide. Not far away, in other cars, were some twenty more of our traveling companions, also being held under guard. Included in that number was my longtime friend, Dr. B. R. Lakin. Knowing him as I did, I knew that he was extremely worried.

The year was 1954, just six years after the founding of the State of Israel. Jerusalem was a divided city having Israeli and Arab sectors, and tensions were high throughout the region. I was delighted to have Dr. Lakin, Dr. Billington and several other friends traveling with me. We had long anticipated this day, thinking that it would be one of the most exciting days of the month-long tour. We were going to the rose-red rock-city of Petra, called *The city that time forgot.*

Early that morning we had left the Jordanian side of Jerusalem. We had been driven to the airport in limousines, where we boarded a plane for Maan, a town in the desert, not many miles from Petra.

The flight passed over a desert waste of mountains and valleys and flat, sandy desert. In about an hour our plane landed at Maan airport. An inordinate amount of time passed before they opened the door of the plane and allowed us to walk down some portable stairs into a circle of armed guards who were not smiling a welcome. They placed all of us under arrest, without bothering to tell us why, and herded us into waiting automobiles. In minutes the cars took off for town with a guard riding in each car.

Dr. Billington and I were fortunate to be placed in the car with our guide, Emil. Since he was an Arab and could speak the language, we hoped he could find out what this was about.

From the minute our car started away from the airport, Emil started talking, and he never stopped. He was angry, too angry for a Christian, I thought, and I was not sure that all the words he used would pass muster in a Sunday school class. When we reached Maan, our driver maneuvered the car along narrow, twisting streets. Emil kept up a heated argument with the driver and the guard. Dr. Billington and I sat quietly, listening to an argument we could not understand. The driver made so many turns, I lost all sense of direction. Finally he swerved from the road and whirled into the barbed wire enclosure that now imprisoned us.

We could hardly have been in a worse predicament. We did not know why we were imprisoned. Our fellow travelers in Jerusalem, who had chosen not to come with us, did not know we were imprisoned, and we had no way to get word to them or to our families in America.

Our guide finally told us that we were being held on the pretense that we were traveling without our passports. The hotel in Jerusalem had taken our passports when we checked in, and they would not return them until we checked out. Our captors knew that perfectly well, but it had not kept them from taking us captive. Besides, we had crossed no borders. We had left Jerusalem, Jordan that morning, and we were now in Maan, Jordan. They did not have a valid charge. Apparently that was the only thing they could come up with.

After a time, they let our guide leave the car to go and talk with someone. When he returned, he told us that they were going to release our car so he could go and confer with the mayor of the city. Of course our armed guard stayed in the car with us.

Our driver took us along several winding streets and made several turns. After about ten miles, he stopped the car beside a large house. Our guide told us to remain in the car while he went in to talk with the mayor. The driver got out with him, but the guard remained in the car with us. I doubt that he remained just to be sociable.

After about a half hour, Emil and the driver returned. "The mayor wants you to come in and partake of his hospitality," Emil told us, holding the door open for us to get out.

We were invited in at the mayor's house and told to be seated. Soon a maid came and offered us coffee and cookies. The coffee was black and strong, as it always is in that part of the world. I had been ill from some infection when I left Jerusalem, and all I had been through had made me feel worse. I feared that if I drank that strong, black coffee, I would really be sick, but if I did not my friends would probably never get out of that barbed wire prison. I decided to make the supreme sacrifice. I drank that thick, strong, coffee—every drop of it.

Either the Lord helped me or the coffee had a medicinal effect, for my stomach stopped hurting at once, and it did not bother me again on the trip.

After that, we were driven back to where our friends were waiting behind barbed wire, and the guards released us and let us go on our way. Despite all that had happened, we had a great adventure seeing and exploring Petra.

Our trip back to Jerusalem was uneventful, but what we went through that day will always remain high on the list of the unforgettable experiences of my life.

How God Put Things Together

In 1961 the IFF (now called the IFFB) was a fledgling organization. Dr. Fred Garland, founder and president, was promoting the IFF with a series of conferences in several states in the southeast and as far west as Phoenix. He asked me to clear three months of my schedule to travel and speak in most of these meetings.

In August, the next year, we were in a conference in the Good News Baptist Church in Norfolk, Virginia, where Dr. D. M. Hardison was then pastor. The big news that week was the building of the Berlin Wall and the efforts of people to escape from Communist-controlled East Berlin. The media was carrying stories of East Berliners crashing through barricades in cars and trucks, jumping over the wall from second story windows, swimming the canal, and crawling through barbed wire entanglements to escape to the West.

One day during the conference, Dr. Garland, an idea man, had one of his sudden bright ideas. "Doctor, why don't you fly to West Berlin and preach to the refugees?" he asked, turning to me. "You can go as the representative of the IFF."

I knew what that meant. The IFF would say, "God Bless you." I knew, and Dr. Garland knew, that the IFF did not have any money. Nonetheless, the idea appealed to me, and I immediately felt that it was the will of the Lord for me to go.

"I will need time to raise money for the trip," I responded.

"How long will it take? You ought to go now."

"I think I can raise money for the trip in two weeks."

The next thing I knew, Dr. Garland had me on the phone talking to Governor A. B. (Happy)

Chandler, then governor of Kentucky, and asking him to pull some wires so I could get into that hot spot of the conflict between the USSR and the United States. I told Governor Chandler that I wanted to preach to the refugees and also to our American servicemen while I was there. Governor Chandler responded that he would take care of it.

I returned home, raised enough money to pay my expenses and borrowed enough for Mrs. Arnold to go with me. Then I called Dr. Garland and told him I was ready to go. "Who is my contact when I get to Berlin, Dr. Garland?" I asked.

"I—I don't—don't know," he answered. "Why, Doctor, I thought you would know somebody."

With a shock, I realized that Dr. Garland had no idea where I was to go or who I was to contact when I got to West Berlin. My heart sank, for I had no more idea how I was to make contacts in Berlin than he did. But I had to go, for many of my friends had given sacrificially so I could go and preach to the refuges. I could not let them down. Besides, I was convinced that the Lord wanted me to go.

After I hung up the phone, I prayed about what to do. Then I phoned Dr. Ford Porter, author of the world-famous tract *God's Simple Plan of Salvation*. When he came on the line, I explained my problem and asked if he had any contacts in West Berlin.

After a moment's thought, he answered, "Well

there's Kurt Wagner. He was a member of Hitler's body guard. He got saved by reading my tract, but he will be two or three hundred miles from where you're going. I don't see how you can get in touch with him." After a pause he continued, "There's another man, a missionary from Indiana, but he will also be at least two hundred miles from where you will be. I'll give you his name anyway, just in case." I wrote down the name, told Dr. Porter good-bye and hung up the phone, realizing that I would have to make the trip by faith.

On the appointed day, Mrs. Arnold and I flew to West Berlin. We deplaned, checked through customs, and walked into the terminal.

"What are we going to do now?" she asked as we set our bags on the floor.

"Wait by the bags while I find someone to talk with."

I had done a considerable amount of praying on the flight across the Atlantic, and I felt that the Lord wanted us to go to the American sector where at least we could find somebody we could talk to. I found my way to a counter and located a man who could speak English, and he told me how to get to the American sector.

I returned to Mrs. Arnold; we picked up our bags and followed the directions I had been given. Some while later we reached the American sector and found ourselves standing on a lonely corner in a foreign city and not knowing where we were to go. Neither of us knew a word of German.

I thought this was a good time to pray, so I bowed my head and prayed for the Lord to direct us. If Mrs. Arnold prayed, she must have prayed with her eyes open. As soon as I ended my prayer, she said, "I just saw an American soldier and a woman go in that store over there." She pointed to a store across the street.

We hurried to the store and found the soldier and his German wife. We explained our problem to them, and they invited us to go home with them so the wife could make some calls on our behalf.

By the time they finished shopping and drove across the city to their home it was late afternoon. The soldier's wife prepared a snack for us and insisted that we eat before she made the phone calls.

After we finished eating, she placed a call to a Lutheran pastor. That would be a useless call, I thought, but it turned out not to be. The Lutheran pastor gave her the phone number of an English missionary and suggested that she call him. She placed that call and explained the situation to the missionary.

"I think we have solved your problem," she said as she hung up. "The missionary said he was just leaving to go to a tent revival. He is coming by here, and he wants you to go to the meeting with him."

I was greatly surprised. The last thing I expected to find in West Berlin was a tent revival.

When the missionary arrived, he had a friend

with him. My surprise knew no bounds when he introduced his friend. He was the missionary from Indiana that Dr. Ford Porter had told me about. The odds against that happening were astronomical. A prayer and two phone calls, and here was the only contact I had in Germany. Only God could have brought us together in this manner.

We soon reached a large tent where a German pastor was holding a meeting. The tent was packed with people. The missionary ushered me to the platform and introduced me to the pastor. The pastor asked me to give my testimony, and I was privileged to speak briefly to the great crowd, through an interpreter.

The next day the English missionary took me to preach to the refugees who had escaped to freedom in the West. I had the joy of telling them that they could have real freedom if they would receive Jesus Christ as Savior. Many of them did.

After preaching in West Berlin for a few days, arrangements were made for me and Mrs. Arnold to go to the Ruhr Valley and work with a German missionary. God blessed our efforts there, and many souls were saved. Those who had risked their lives to find freedom in the West found real freedom in Christ. Only God could have worked out the arrangement for me to make the contacts that immediately opened those doors for me.

Chapter 23
Looking to the Future

*Y*ears ago Solomon wrote: *"Who is she that looketh forth as the morning, fair as the moon, clear as the sun, and terrible as an army with banners?"* (Song of Solomon 6:10).

Morning time is the time of planning and looking forward to the opportunities of the day. The morning time of life is also a time of planning, of dreams, and of visions. It is unfortunate that as we grow older we often lose sight of our dreams and begin to live in the past.

In our youth, our emotions were strong and our excitement was easily aroused. As a result much of what happened was indelibly stamped in memory. So memories of our past are our strongest memories, and they are the ones that stay with us through life. When we come to the place in life where nothing exciting is happening, we retain few memories of day to day events. Since we have so few recent memories, it is natural for us to go back and relive the exciting, happy memories of the past.

That is a pleasant way to spend our time, but

we should not spend so much time reminiscing that we let the remaining days of our lives pass us by with few worthwhile achievements. As we grow older, if we have health and energy, life can still be exciting, productive, and rewarding.

Oops, I forgot I'm not supposed to be preaching. I'm supposed to be writing about the way things used to be. And I am, sort of. But when you look back to the way things used to be, isn't that looking back to the past? Of course it is, and there's nothing wrong with recalling those treasured memories of long ago, as long as we don't get stuck back there. I try hard not to do that. I enjoy recalling those happy days of long ago, but I keep focused on what I plan to do in the future.

I like to keep in mind the words of Paul, the Apostle. *". . . but this one thing I do, forgetting those things which are behind, and reaching forth unto those things which are before, I press toward the mark for the prize of the high calling of God in Christ Jesus"* (Phil. 3:13,14).

At the beginning of each new year, I make a New Year's dedication, and I ask the Lord to help me to serve Him better than I did in the preceding year. Also, I ask Him to help me accomplish more in His service than in any previous year.

I cannot relive the years that are gone. I cannot do again the things I used to do, but I can do things now that I could not have done back then. The coming days of my life will offer new opportunities and challenges, and with God's help, I want to make the most of them. I frequently pray that the Lord will make my remaining days the most productive days of my life.

I have no way of knowing how long I will live in this world, but I do not plan to die to life and service as long as I am able to walk, and think, and work. I have too many things to do for me to die before the Lord gets through with me. Even when my time comes, as Dr. Lakin used to say, "I'll be holding onto the willow bushes."

While I'm working at present tasks, I keep many things in mind that I want to do in the future. One of the thing I plan to do is write more books. Writing books involves more time and work than I ever dreamed possible, but writing them keeps me busy and excited. And I know that my books are being used by the Lord to bless many lives.

One day my body will wear out, and I will not be able to do as much as I am presently doing. But I do not plan to hasten that day by allowing my body to rust out. I believe in keeping busy. I believe in exercising my body and keep my muscles strong. I do several kinds of aerobic exercise most every day. I'm not above manual labor. I raise a garden each year. I do repair work on our buildings, and occasionally I chop wood. I would do more of that sort of thing if time permitted. I avoid a couch and an easy chair like the plague. I believe rocking chairs have killed more people than shovels ever have. I eat a healthful diet. I take vitamins, and sometimes minerals and herbs. I try to drink enough water, and I insist on getting enough sleep. I have learned that I function better if my body is not walking around starved for sleep.

If the time comes when I am no longer able to work, I will do all I can to keep my mind active. And I will still look to the future. There is no end of life for a Christian. We will experience a transition, but that will not end consciousness.

One day I will reach the end of my journey on earth. I know not whether it will be at the Coming of the Lord or at the breaking of the wheel at the fountain, as Solomon puts it in Ecclesiastes. I know that one day I will leave this world and go to a world where there are no tears and no good-byes.

I have often wondered just how my transition will take place. Perhaps the Lord will come again in my lifetime, and I will be caught up with my loved ones and friends to meet Him in the air. Or, it may be that I will wear my body out—that one day I will walk my last mile across a field and pause at the bank of a river. It may be that my friends and family will walk with me down to the riverbank, and I will have time to tell them good-bye. Their hands may hold my hand until the clasp is broken and I slide into the river.

For a fleeting moment, I may feel that I am adrift in the Jordan of death. Then I will feel a hand clasp mine, and I will know that it is the hand of my Savior. Perhaps He will bear me across the river. Or He may lift me to my feet, and I will walk with Him on the surface of the river as Peter walked with Him on the waves of storm-tossed Galilee. In either case, we will soon step upon the shore of Immanuel's Land, and I will know I am home at last.

I will fall at the feet of Jesus and worship Him. Then He will lift me up and point to a city on a hill. People will be pouring out of the gates of the city and trooping down the hillside to meet me, and I will hear them shouting, "Welcome home! Welcome home, thou redeemed in the blood of the Lamb!"

And I will echo, "Home at last! Home at last!" That will be the first minute of the unending day of my new life of service for the Lord, who loved me and washed me from my sins.

Of course I look forward to seeing my loved ones in that land where we shall know as we also are known. There will be no parting over there and no sad good-byes. In that land where there is no night, we will never grow tired or weary. We will have time for each other. We will have time to worship and praise our Lord, and we will have time to do all the things we did not have time to do on earth. Eternity! Oh, eternity! *And whosoever liveth and believeth in me shall never die*" (John 11:25). Amen, and Amen.

Comments On L. Walker Arnold Novels
By His Readers

"Your book was the best book I ever read." Salesgirl, Tennessee.

"What a book! It is one of the best books I've read since Grace Livingston Hill's day." Lady, Columbia, Kentucky.

"I loved your book, *Out of the Night*. I laughed and cried and rejoiced as I read it." Lady. Lexington, Kentucky.

"There was no way I could lay *The Legend of Old Faithful* down. At 1:00 a.m.." Pastor's Wife, Florida.

"I've read *The Legend of Old Faithful* twice, and I'm going to read it again." Lady, Kentucky.

"*Out of the Night*, is the best book I ever read. I couldn't put it down." Retired coal miner, Beckley, West Virginia.

"My 15-year-old daughter read *The Legend,* and she enjoyed it thoroughly." Lady, Elkview, West Virginia.

"I received my copy of *Fathoms Deep*, and read it immediately. I can't wait for your next book." Pastor's wife, Norwood, Ohio.

"After reading *Fathoms Deep*, I wished I had another one to read." Lady, Lexington, Kentucky.

"Yes—yes—yes. I would like three copies of *Fathoms Deep*. Send two copies to the enclosed addresses and one to my address.." Lady, Central City, Kentucky.

"We have your first two books, *The Legend of Old Faithful*

over

and *Out of the Night.* The same people come in and check them out again and again to reread them. We are glad to get your new book." Librarian, McCreary County, Kentucky.

"I enjoyed *Out of the Night* very much. I was amazed at your ability to describe the downtown area of Knoxville. We used to live there." Man, Knoxville, Tennessee.

"That book, *Riverman,* is the best book you have written. Put me down for the next book." Lady, Lexington, Kentucky.

"I was intrigued by *Riverman.* Your description is so graphic and your characters were so real, I felt that I had made some new friends." Professor's wife, Wilmore, Kentucky.

"I have *Sunshine Valley.* I am not one to read books, but I read every word of this one and really enjoyed it." Pastor' wife, Dundee, Florida.

"I have read four of your books and enjoyed them all but especially *Euroclydon!* The story made the Bible so real and helped me to understand what life was like in A. D. 60. I felt like I was there." Lady, Michigan City, Indiana.

"*Euroclydon* was interesting from beginning to end. I wish I didn't have to wait so long until the next book is ready." Lady, Richmond, Kentucky.

"I just read *Lucinda of Perryville.* It is your greatest book yet. I love it. I could read it a hundred times." Lady, Lexington, Kentucky.

"I have enjoyed all your books, but I think *Lucinda of Perryville* is the best yet. Hope you are now writing another." Lady, Wichita, Kansas.

L. Walker Arnold

A Beloved Christian Author

Since 1986, when L. Walker Arnold's first novel, *The Legend of Old Faithful*, was published, he has become one of America's best loved authors. His readers frequently write that they read his books over and over, and they complain that he is only writing one book each year.

From the time the title of a new book he is working on is announced, his readers start placing their orders for it. Hundreds of advance orders are received before the book is off the press.

Interestingly, and he says, much to his surprise, the mere reading of one of his books usually turns his readers into potential customers. They often go to great pains to locate his books, even writing to one of his publishers to ask where they can buy them. We suggest that those who are attempting to locate his books ask their bookstore to stock them. If that is not possible, all of his books may be ordered from Arnold Publications.

Arnold Publications
2440 Bethel Road
Nicholasville, KY 40356

Or phone toll free: 1-800-854-8571

Don't Miss These Great L. Walker Arnold Novels

In the past few years L. Walker Arnold, a native of Kentucky, has become a widely-read, greatly-loved inspirational author.

He has written seven novels and his life story, *The Way Things Used to Be* in the past nine years. All of them have been well received by the reading public.

Hundreds of his readers order each of his new books long before it is off the press. Many have placed standing orders for every book he writes. Thousands have written to praise his books.

Mr. Arnold's readers write that they appreciate his ability to create strong characters, his unique powers of description, and the gripping, emotion-filled stories he writes.

Titles Listed in the Order Written

The Legend of Old Faithful, Hardcover	$15.99
Out of the Night, Hardcover	$15.99
Fathoms Deep, Hardcover	$15.99
Riverman, Softcover	$ 9.99
Riverman (Audio) read by author on cassette	$12.99
White Angel, Paperbound	$ 1.00
Sunshine Valley, Softcover	$ 9.99
Euroclydon, Softcover	$ 9.99
Lucinda of Perryville, Softcover	$ 9.99

If L. Walker Arnold novels are not available at bookstores in your area, order from Arnold Publications.

Please include $2.00 postage and handling for one book, $3.00 for two books, $3.50 for three books, $4.00 for four books, and $4.50 for five books. We pay postage on orders over $50.00. Prices are subject to change without notice.

Arnold Publications
2440 Bethel Road
Nicholasville, KY 40356

Phone toll free 1-800-854-8571